For more than 50 years, *The Australian Women's Weekly* Test Kitchen has been creating marvellous recipes that come with a guarantee of success. First, the recipes always work — just follow the instructions and you too will get the results you see in the photographs. Second, and perhaps more importantly, they are delicious — created by experienced home economists and chefs, all triple-tested and, thanks to their straightforward instructions, easy to make.

British and North American readers:
Please note that Australian cup and
spoon measurements are metric.
A quick conversion guide appears
on page 119.

We're a nation hooked on seafood – never before in our history have we consumed so much of so many varieties cooked in so many different ways – and why not? Quick and easy to prepare, a great source of protein and good oils, versatile enough to cross all culinary borders: seafood simply and deliciously has insinuated itself into our quest for a healthy lifestyle.

In *The Essential Seafood Cookbook*, you'll not only be able to choose from a stunning array of recipes but you'll also learn how to tell your anchovies from your yabbies, plus gain confidence in purchasing and expertise in preparing crustaceans and molluscs as well as fish. Take the plunge – dive into the pages of this book and discover the mouthwatering appeal of scrumptious seafood.

Pamela Clark

FOOD EDITOR

contents

fish

Slow-roasted, fast-fried or steamed, fish lends itself to almost as many cooking methods as there are people to invent them. Its adaptability, forgiving texture and delicate yet distinctive flavour make fish a universally loved food – and, even better, one of the more healthy ones.

garfish with leek, prosciutto and prawns

PREPARATION TIME 35 MINUTES • COOKING TIME 15 MINUTES

You could substitute sardines in this recipe; adjust the number of fish.

Boning garfish

Flattening fish with rolling pin

Rolling fish to enclose prawn

1 medium leek (350g)
12 large cooked
prawns (250g)
12 garfish (820g),
butterflied (see page 110)
12 slices prosciutto (190g)
1/4 cup roasted vegetable
pesto (70g)
2 medium yellow
zucchini (240g)
2 medium green
zucchini (240g)

1 Cut leek in half lengthways; cut into 10cm lengths. Separate layers. Drop leek into pan of boiling water; drain, rinse under cold water, drain.

2 Shell and devein prawns, leaving tails intact (see page 111).

3 Flatten garfish with rolling pin, place fish skin-side down on board; line with pieces of leek, then prosciutto. Spread with 1 teaspoon pesto, top with prawn. Starting from head of fish, roll to enclose prawn; secure with toothpick. Repeat with remaining ingredients. *[Can be made ahead to this stage. Cover, refrigerate overnight].*

4 Cut zucchini lengthways into 5mm-thick slices. Cook on heated oiled grill plate (or grill or barbecue) until browned and tender; cover, keep warm.

5 Cook fish on heated oiled grill plate (or grill or barbecue) until cooked through. Serve fish with char-grilled zucchini.

SERVES 4

per serve 10g fat; 1246kJ
serving suggestion Serve with a mixed green salad.

tip Roasted vegetable pesto is available from most supermarkets; alternatively, you can use your favourite pesto.

tempura platter

PREPARATION TIME 30 MINUTES • COOKING TIME 15 MINUTES

200g squid hoods
2 flathead fillets (200g)
20 medium uncooked
 prawns (500g)
1 small brown onion (80g)
2 eggs
1¹/₂ cups iced water (375ml)
1 cup plain flour (150g)
1 cup cornflour (150g)
vegetable oil, for deep-frying
1 small kumara (250g),
 sliced thinly
100g snow peas
150g fresh shiitake
 mushrooms, halved
1 large carrot (180g),
 grated coarsely
1 medium potato (200g),
 grated coarsely
2 tablespoons lime juice
2 tablespoons soy sauce
2 tablespoons sweet
 chilli sauce

1 Cut squid into 1cm rings, cut fish into 3cm pieces; shell and devein prawns, leaving tails intact (see page 111).

2 Cut onion into 4 wedges; separate wedges into pieces 3 or 4 layers thick, secure with toothpicks.

3 Just before serving, whisk eggs and the water together in medium bowl; stir in sifted flours all at once. Do not over-mix; mixture should be lumpy.

4 Heat oil in large pan. Dip seafood, onion, kumara, snow peas and mushrooms, in batches, into batter; deep-fry until browned lightly and cooked through. Drain on absorbent paper, keep warm.

5 Stir combined carrot and potato into remaining batter; deep-fry tablespoons of mixture, in batches, until browned lightly. Drain on absorbent paper.

6 Serve seafood and vegetables with combined remaining ingredients as a dipping sauce.

SERVES 4

per serve 4.7g fat; 1745kJ (excludes oil for deep-frying)

Deep-frying carrot and potato mixture

pepper-roasted barramundi

PREPARATION TIME 25 MINUTES • COOKING TIME 35 MINUTES

You can use any small, whole, white-fleshed fish for this recipe. Sichuan or anise peppercorns have a hot, aromatic flavour and are used in Chinese five-spice powder and oriental dishes.

4 small whole barramundi (1.2kg)
2 tablespoons Sichuan peppercorns
1/2 teaspoon five-spice powder
1/2 teaspoon salt
1/4 cup lime juice (60ml)
1/4 cup peanut oil (60ml)
200g dried rice stick noodles
100g fresh shiitake mushrooms,
   sliced thinly
1kg baby bok choy, trimmed
40g fresh ginger, sliced thinly
1/3 cup oyster sauce (80ml)
2 teaspoons sesame oil
1/4 cup water (60ml)

1 Score each fish both sides; place on large piece of foil. Finely crush peppercorns, add spice and salt. Combine spice mixture with juice and 1 tablespoon of the peanut oil in small bowl, brush mixture over each fish. Wrap foil securely around each fish; place on oven tray. Cook in moderately hot oven for about 20 minutes or until fish are cooked through.

2 Meanwhile, place noodles in large heatproof bowl, cover with boiling water, stand until just tender; drain. Toss noodles with 1 tablespoon of the peanut oil.

3 Heat remaining peanut oil in wok or large pan; stir-fry mushrooms until browned. Add bok choy and ginger; stir-fry until bok choy is just wilted. Add noodles, sauce, sesame oil and the water; stir-fry until heated through. Serve with the roasted fish.

SERVES 4

per serve 23g fat; 2264kJ

Scoring fish

Crushing peppercorns with a meat mallet

bouillabaisse

PREPARATION TIME 1 HOUR • COOKING TIME 3 HOURS

While the fish stock and rouille can be made a day ahead and kept, covered, in the refrigerator, the bouillabaisse should be made and served immediately, as seafood does not reheat successfully.

**20 medium uncooked
prawns (500g)**
300g squid hoods
1kg redfish fillets
**500g mussels, prepared
(see page 112)**
200g cooked crab meat

FISH STOCK

4 fish heads
2.5 litres water (10 cups)
1 tablespoon olive oil
**1 medium leek (350g),
sliced thinly**
**1 large brown onion (200g),
sliced thinly**
2 cloves garlic, crushed
**3 large tomatoes (750g),
peeled, chopped finely**
1/4 cup tomato paste (60ml)
1/4 teaspoon fennel seeds
1 bay leaf
pinch saffron threads

ROUILLE

1 clove garlic, quartered
1 red Thai chilli, seeded, chopped
1/2 cup olive oil (125ml)
1 cup stale breadcrumbs (70g)
1 tablespoon tomato paste

1 Shell and devein prawns, leaving tails intact (see page 111); discard heads, reserve shells. Cover prawns; refrigerate until required.

2 Make fish stock; keep hot.

3 Cut squid into 1cm rings; cut fish into 4cm pieces. Add seafood to stock; do not boil, simmer, covered, 10 minutes or until seafood changes colour and mussels open. Discard any mussels that do not open. Serve bouillabaisse topped with rouille.

fish stock Combine reserved prawn shells, fish heads and the water in large pan; bring to boil, simmer, covered, 20 minutes. Strain fish liquid through muslin-lined sieve over large heatproof bowl; discard solids. Heat oil in large pan; cook leek, onion and garlic, stirring, until onion is soft. Add the fish liquid, tomato, paste, seeds, bay leaf and saffron; bring to boil, simmer, covered, 2 hours. Remove bay leaf, discard; reserve 1/4 cup stock for rouille.

rouille Blend or process garlic, chilli and 1 tablespoon of the oil until chopped finely. Add breadcrumbs and reserved fish stock; process until almost smooth, add tomato paste. With motor operating, add remaining oil in thin stream; process until rouille thickens.

SERVES 6

per serve 30g fat; 2383kJ

Straining fish liquid

Adding tomato paste to rouille

walnut gremolata bream

PREPARATION TIME 25 MINUTES • COOKING TIME 30 MINUTES

*Gremolata is a traditional Italian garnish usually made of finely chopped fresh
parsley, lemon rind and garlic. You can use any small white fish fillets for this recipe.*

Chopping lemon rind

1 Combine nuts, rind, parsley and
half the garlic in small bowl;
cover gremolata.

2 Boil, steam or microwave
potato until tender; drain.
Mash potato with butter,
milk and remaining garlic.

3 Meanwhile, brush fish with
oil; cook, skin-side down first,
on heated oiled grill plate
(or pan-fry) until browned on
both sides and cooked through.

4 Serve fish on garlic mash;
sprinkle with gremolata.

SERVES 4

per serve 24.9g fat; 1964kJ
tip Garlic mash can be made
ahead; keep covered in
refrigerator. Reheat garlic
mash, covered, in microwave
oven on MEDIUM (55%) about
3 minutes, stirring twice.

**1/3 cup walnut pieces (35g),
toasted, chopped finely**
**2 tablespoons finely chopped
lemon rind**
**1/4 cup finely chopped
fresh parsley**
2 cloves garlic, crushed

**4 medium potatoes
(800g), quartered**
40g butter, chopped
1/4 cup milk (60ml)
4 bream fillets (640g)
1 tablespoon olive oil

thai green curry fish

PREPARATION TIME 30 MINUTES • COOKING TIME 15 MINUTES

You can use any firm-fleshed fish fillets or cutlets for this recipe.

750g ling fillets

1 tablespoon peanut oil

1 clove garlic, crushed

**1 tablespoon finely chopped
    fresh lemon grass**

**1 red Thai chilli, seeded,
    chopped finely**

**1/4 cup Thai-style green curry
    paste (70g)**

1²/₃ cups coconut cream (400ml)

1 cup vegetable stock (250ml)

2 green onions, chopped finely

**350g snake beans,
    chopped coarsely**

**1 tablespoon finely grated
    lime rind**

**2 tablespoons finely chopped
    fresh coriander leaves**

**1 small red capsicum (150g),
    chopped finely**

**1/4 cup finely chopped
    toasted macadamias (35g)**

1 Cut fish into 3cm pieces.

2 Heat oil in large pan; cook garlic, lemon grass, chilli and paste, stirring, until fragrant. Stir in cream and stock; bring to boil.

3 Add fish, onion and beans; simmer, covered, until fish is cooked through and beans are tender.

4 Combine rind, coriander, capsicum and nuts in small bowl; sprinkle over curry.

SERVES 4

per serve 40.8g fat; 2475kJ

serving suggestion Serve curry with boiled or steamed basmati or jasmine rice.

Chopping snake beans

cantonese steamed gingered snapper

PREPARATION TIME 10 MINUTES • COOKING TIME 40 MINUTES

If snapper is unavailable, use your favourite whole firm-fleshed fish for this recipe.

40g piece ginger
1 large whole snapper (1.2kg)
1/4 cup vegetable stock (60ml)
4 green onions, sliced thinly
1/2 cup tightly packed fresh coriander leaves, chopped coarsely
1/3 cup light soy sauce (80ml)
1 teaspoon sesame oil

1 Peel ginger; cut into thin strips lengthways, then cut into matchstick-size pieces.

2 Score fish three times both sides; place on large sheet of foil, sprinkle with half the ginger and drizzle with half of the vegetable stock, fold foil loosely to enclose fish.

3 Place fish in large bamboo steamer; steam fish, covered, over wok or pan of simmering water about 40 minutes or until cooked through.

4 Transfer fish to serving dish; sprinkle with remaining ginger, onion, coriander, then drizzle with combined remaining stock, sauce and oil.

SERVES 4

per serve 5.6g fat; 1224kJ

serving suggestion Serve with fried rice, and stir-fried bok choy with ginger and garlic.

Cutting ginger into "matchsticks"

Placing fish in steamer

Squeezing excess water from bread

1 Cook fish, uncovered, in heated oiled grill pan (or on grill or barbecue) until just cooked through.

2 Heat the oil in large pan; cook spinach, stirring, until just wilted.

3 Divide skordalia among serving plates; top with fish, spinach and combined yogurt, mint and juice.

skordalia Boil, steam or microwave potato until tender; drain. Mash potato in large bowl with garlic. Trim and discard crusts from bread; soak bread in small bowl of cold water. Drain, squeeze excess water from bread; add bread to potato mixture, beat until smooth. Gradually add combined oil, juice and vinegar; beat until smooth.

SERVES 4

per serve 26g fat; 2069kJ

serving suggestion Preceded by a mezze of dolmades (filled vine leaves), cubes of fetta and kalamata olives, this main course becomes an authentic Greek meal.

tip Skordalia is traditionally served with dishes including grilled meats, poultry, fish, soups, and as a dip for raw vegetables and/or bread.

swordfish with skordalia

PREPARATION TIME 10 MINUTES • COOKING TIME 25 MINUTES

You can substitute tuna steaks or cutlets for swordfish.

4 swordfish steaks (800g)
2 teaspoons olive oil
500g baby spinach leaves
1/3 cup yogurt (80ml)
1 teaspoon finely chopped fresh mint leaves
2 teaspoons lemon juice

SKORDALIA

2 medium potatoes (400g), chopped coarsely
6 cloves garlic, crushed
2 slices stale white bread
1/3 cup olive oil (80ml)
1 tablespoon lemon juice
1 tablespoon white wine vinegar

lime and tamarind bream

PREPARATION TIME 20 MINUTES • COOKING TIME 30 MINUTES

You can use any small, whole, white-fleshed fish for this recipe.

**2 tablespoons thick
tamarind concentrate**
1/3 cup boiling water (80ml)
2 cloves garlic, crushed
**1 tablespoon grated
fresh ginger**
2 tablespoons lime juice
**2 red Thai chillies, seeded,
chopped finely**

**2 tablespoons finely
chopped lemon grass**
16 kaffir lime leaves, torn
**4 medium whole
bream (1.8kg)**
**1/2 cup loosely packed
fresh coriander leaves**
**2 red Thai chillies, sliced
thinly, extra**

1 Combine tamarind concentrate
and the water in medium bowl;
stir in garlic, ginger, juice,
chilli and lemon grass.

2 Divide lime leaves among fish
cavities. Score fish both sides;
brush with one-third of the
tamarind mixture.

3 Wrap each fish in foil, place on
oven tray; cook in moderately
hot oven about 30 minutes
or until fish is cooked through,
brushing with more of the
tamarind mixture during
cooking. Serve fish topped
with coriander and extra
sliced chillies.

SERVES 4

per serve 11.7g fat; 1207kJ
serving suggestion Serve with
boiled rice.

tip Use tamarind pulp if you
cannot locate the concentrate
– soak 100g tamarind pulp in
1/2 cup hot water for 10 minutes;
squeeze pulp to release extra
flavour. Strain; use liquid,
discard pulp.

Placing leaves in cavity of fish

slow-roasted salmon with asian greens

PREPARATION TIME 15 MINUTES • COOKING TIME 40 MINUTES

750g piece salmon fillet, boned, with skin on
1 fresh kaffir lime, quartered
1 tablespoon finely shredded kaffir lime leaves
1/2 cup caster sugar (110g)
1/4 cup lime juice (60ml)
1/4 cup water (60ml)
2 red Thai chillies, seeded, chopped finely
1/4 cup tightly packed fresh coriander leaves, chopped finely
1 tablespoon peanut oil
250g fresh asparagus, trimmed, chopped coarsely
150g snow peas
150g baby bok choy, chopped coarsely
150g choy sum, chopped coarsely

1 Cook fish and quartered lime on heated oiled grill plate (or grill or barbecue) until both are lightly coloured all over. Place fish and lime in oiled large baking dish; sprinkle with lime leaves. Bake, covered tightly, in very slow oven about 30 minutes or until cooked as desired.

2 Meanwhile, combine sugar, juice and the water in small pan; stir over heat, without boiling, until sugar dissolves. Simmer, uncovered, without stirring, 3 minutes; cool slightly. Stir in chilli and coriander.

3 Heat the oil in wok or large pan; stir-fry asparagus and snow peas until just tender. Add bok choy and choy sum with half of the chilli sauce; stir-fry until leaves are just wilted.

4 Serve vegetables with fish, drizzled with remaining chilli sauce.

SERVES 4

per serve 16.3g fat; 1686kJ

Grilling fish and lime wedges

Stir-frying vegetables and sauce

red emperor with pecan rice

PREPARATION TIME 20 MINUTES • COOKING TIME 45 MINUTES

If you do not have access to a banana tree, you can buy fresh banana leaves from supermarkets or fruit and vegetable stores, already cleaned and cut into manageable pieces. You can use any whole, firm, white-fleshed fish.

GREY BOWL FROM EMPIRE HOMEWARES

Securing leaves with string

2 banana leaves
1 whole red emperor (1.2kg)
1 teaspoon peanut oil
1 teaspoon red wine vinegar

PECAN RICE

1/2 x 375g packet
  wild rice blend
1/2 cup pecans (50g), toasted,
  chopped coarsely
1 medium tomato (190g),
  seeded, sliced thinly
2 green onions, sliced thinly
1 tablespoon red wine vinegar
1 tablespoon lemon juice

1 Cut banana leaves into pieces large enough to fit into a large pan of boiling water. Using tongs, dip one piece of leaf at a time into boiling water; remove, rinse under cold water, pat dry with absorbent paper. Leaves should be soft and pliable.

2 Overlap pieces of banana leaf to form one rectangle about twice as long as the fish and three times as wide. Score fish three times on each side; brush with combined oil and vinegar. Place fish on banana leaves; fill fish cavity with pecan rice.

3 Fold leaves over fish; secure with kitchen string.

4 Place fish on lightly oiled oven tray, bake in very hot oven about 30 minutes or until fish is cooked through. Serve fish with any remaining rice mixture.

pecan rice Cook rice in large pan of boiling water, uncovered, about 15 minutes or until just tender; drain. Combine rice with remaining ingredients in large bowl.

SERVES 4

per serve 19g fat; 1872kJ

grilled cutlets with artichokes

PREPARATION TIME 10 MINUTES • COOKING TIME 20 MINUTES

You can use any firm white-fleshed fish cutlets for this recipe. Any commercially made pesto based on basil is suitable.

2/3 cup basil pesto (160ml)

1 cup firmly packed fresh basil leaves

2 x 400g cans artichoke hearts, drained, halved

1 large red onion (300g), sliced thinly

2 large mushrooms (300g), peeled, sliced thickly

2 baby eggplants (120g), sliced lengthways

4 blue-eye cutlets (1kg)

1/2 cup firmly packed shredded fresh basil leaves, extra

1 Blend or process pesto and basil until combined; reserve 1/4 cup pesto mixture.

2 Combine artichoke, onion, mushroom, eggplant and half of the remaining pesto mixture in large bowl.

3 Cook vegetables and mushroom on heated oiled grill plate (or grill or barbecue) until browned and tender; cover, keep warm.

4 Brush fish with reserved 1/4 cup pesto mixture. Cook fish on heated oiled grill plate (or grill or barbecue) until cooked through.

5 Combine remaining pesto mixture, extra basil and char-grilled vegetables in large bowl.

6 Divide vegetables among serving plates; top with fish.

SERVES 4

per serve 19.4g fat; 2039kJ

Blending pesto and basil in food processor

Cooking vegetables on grill plate

lemon and garlic kebabs with puy lentils

PREPARATION TIME 25 MINUTES • COOKING TIME 30 MINUTES

Puy lentils are distinctive by their small size, dark green colour, firmness and quick cooking time. Originally from Le Puy in France and available from gourmet food stores,. they retain their shape well. Any firm-fleshed fish fillets are suitable.

¹/₂ cup puy lentils (100g)
500g red mullet fillets
50g butter, softened
2 cloves garlic, crushed
2 teaspoons finely grated lemon rind
1 tablespoon finely chopped fresh chives
1 large zucchini (150g), chopped finely
1 large carrot (180g), chopped finely
1 medium red capsicum (200g), chopped finely

1 Cook lentils in large pan of boiling water, uncovered, about 15 minutes or until just tender; drain.

2 Meanwhile, remove fish skin; cut fish lengthways, down each side of row of bones, discard bones. Thread fish onto 12 skewers.

3 Combine butter, garlic, rind and chives in small bowl. Place half of the butter mixture in heated large pan. Cover remaining butter mixture; freeze. Add zucchini, carrot and capsicum to pan; cook, stirring, until vegetables are just tender. Add lentils; cook, stirring, until heated through.

4 Cook fish on skewers on heated oiled grill plate (or grill or barbecue) until browned and cooked through. Serve skewers on lentil mixture. Top with thin slices of remaining cold butter mixture.

SERVES 4

per serve 18.5g fat; 1454kJ

tip You need to soak bamboo skewers in water at least 1 hour before using to avoid scorching.

Cutting fish lengthways

Threading fish onto skewers

Trimming celeriac

kingfish with celeriac

PREPARATION TIME 25 MINUTES (PLUS COOLING TIME)
COOKING TIME 1 HOUR

You can use any firm white-fleshed fish fillets for this recipe.

1kg celeriac, trimmed,
  chopped coarsely
4 unpeeled garlic cloves
1 tablespoon olive oil
60g butter
2/3 cup cream (160ml)

2 small leeks (400g)
30g butter, extra
1/2 cup slivered
  almonds (70g)
4 kingfish fillets (1.2kg)

1 Coat celeriac and unpeeled garlic with the oil in large baking dish. Bake, uncovered, in moderate oven about 45 minutes or until celeriac is tender. Cool 10 minutes. Place celeriac in processor; squeeze in pulp from garlic cloves. Add butter, oil from baking dish and cream; process until smooth. Cover to keep warm.

2 Cut leeks into 10cm lengths; halve lengthways, slice thinly. Heat extra butter in large pan, add almonds; cook, stirring, until golden brown. Remove from pan, drain on absorbent paper. Add leeks to same pan; cook, stirring, until soft. Cover to keep warm.

3 Meanwhile, cook fish on heated oiled grill plate (or grill or barbecue) until browned both sides and cooked through. Divide celeriac puree among serving plates; top with fish and combined leek and almonds.

SERVES 4

per serve 51.8g fat; 2957kJ

tip Generally in season during the winter, celeriac is a thick tuberous root, its flavour a combination of celery and potato. It makes an excellent mash, and can also be eaten raw (grated or shredded), or baked or boiled.

steamed lemon-myrtle sand whiting

PREPARATION TIME 10 MINUTES (PLUS STANDING TIME) • COOKING TIME 30 MINUTES

You can substitute your favourite small whole fish.

**2 teaspoons ground
lemon myrtle**
**3/4 cup sweet chilli
sauce (180ml)**
**2 tablespoons finely
grated lime rind**
2 tablespoons lime juice
8 whole sand whiting (1.6kg)
**1/4 cup tightly packed
fresh coriander leaves**

1 Combine lemon myrtle, chilli
sauce, rind and juice in medium
bowl, cover; refrigerate 3 hours
or overnight.

2 Reserve 1/4 cup sauce mixture
for serving. Dip three fish, one
at a time, in remaining sauce
mixture to coat; place in single
layer in large bamboo steamer.
Brush fish with a little remaining
sauce; steam, covered, over wok
or pan of simmering water about
10 minutes or until fish are
cooked through. Remove from
steamer; cover to keep warm.
Repeat with remaining fish
in batches.

3 Drizzle fish with reserved
sauce; sprinkle with coarsely
chopped coriander.

SERVES 4

per serve 2.6g fat; 943kJ

tip We used commercially
packaged ground lemon myrtle,
made from the leaves of a
rainforest tree now farmed on the
east coast of Australia, for this
recipe. If unavailable, substitute
1 teaspoon finely chopped fresh
lemon grass, 1/2 teaspoon finely
grated lime rind and 1 teaspoon
finely grated lemon rind for the
ground mixture.

Combining sauce ingredients

Brushing fish with sauce

batters

The amounts of batter given in each of these recipes will coat 8 medium-sized pieces of fish.

batters and deep-frying

- Most batters improve and thicken slightly if kept in refrigerator for 30 minutes, however Tempura batter should be made just before it is used.
- Have surface of food as dry as possible, so that the batter adheres well to it.
- Fish and seafood should be fried at 175°C to 188°C (350°F to 370°F).
- To check temperature of oil, drop in a 1cm cube of bread; it should brown almost immediately.
- Fry food in small batches so that oil temperature remains constant and the batter is crisp.
- Lower food into pan using tongs or slotted spoon.
- Double-frying is useful for large pieces of fish. First, cook at lower temperature until fish is cooked through; drain. Heat oil to a higher temperature; cook fish again until batter is golden.
- Serve fried food as soon as possible. To keep it hot, place in single layer on oven tray covered with absorbent paper. Cover food loosely with foil; slash holes in foil to allow steam to escape. Place in moderate oven.

basic batter

PREPARATION TIME 5 MINUTES

1 cup self-raising flour (150g)
1 egg
1 cup milk (250ml)

Place flour in medium bowl, make well in centre; add egg. Add milk gradually while whisking; whisk until mixture is smooth. Batter can be made in a blender or processor; blend or process until all ingredients are smooth.

beer batter

PREPARATION TIME 5 MINUTES

1 cup plain flour (150g)
1¹/₄ cups beer (310ml)

Whisk ingredients in medium bowl until smooth.

tip Flat or fresh beer can be used in this recipe.

coconut beer batter

PREPARATION TIME 5 MINUTES

1 cup plain flour (150g)
1¹/₄ cups beer (310ml)
2 tablespoons desiccated coconut

Whisk ingredients in medium bowl until well combined.

tip Flat or fresh beer can be used in this recipe.

tempura batter

PREPARATION TIME 5 MINUTES

1 egg white
1 cup iced water (250ml)
1 cup plain flour (150g), sifted
¹/₄ teaspoon bicarbonate soda

Whisk egg white in small bowl until soft peaks form; gently fold into combined remaining ingredients. Batter should be slightly lumpy. Use batter immediately.

opposite: prawns in coconut beer batter (*above left*); fish pieces in beer batter (*above right*); seafood and vegetables in tempura batter (*below left*); onion rings in basic batter (*below right*)

tuna nori rolls

PREPARATION TIME 35 MINUTES • COOKING TIME 15 MINUTES (PLUS STANDING TIME)

Here's a very popular type of sushi you can easily make at home. Koshihikari rice, grown locally, is available at some supermarkets; you can substitute white short-grain rice, cooked by the absorption method. Any sashimi-quality tuna is suitable. Note that the fish in this recipe is uncooked.

2 cups koshihikari rice (400g)

1/3 cup rice vinegar (80ml)

2 tablespoons sugar

1/4 teaspoon salt

6 sheets toasted nori

120g yellowfin sashimi tuna, sliced thinly

1 Lebanese cucumber (130g), seeded, sliced thinly

1 small avocado (200g), sliced thinly

2 tablespoons pickled ginger slices

1/2 teaspoon wasabi

1 Add rice to large pan of boiling water; boil, uncovered, until just tender. Drain, stand rice 5 minutes; stir in combined vinegar, sugar and salt. Cool.

2 Place one sheet of nori, rough-side up, on damp bamboo sushi mat. Dip fingers in water and spread one-sixth of the rice mixture over nori, leaving a 4cm strip on short side closest to you; press rice firmly in place. Using a finger, make a lengthways hollow across centre of rice. Place one-sixth of each of the tuna, cucumber, avocado, ginger and wasabi in hollow across centre of rice.

3 Starting at edge closest to you, use mat to help roll the tuna nori, pressing firmly as you roll. Remove mat from finished nori roll. Cut roll into 6 pieces and place on serving plate; repeat with remaining ingredients.

4 Serve tuna nori rolls with soy sauce, and extra pickled ginger and wasabi, if desired.

MAKES 36 PIECES

per 6 pieces 6.3g fat; 1453kJ

tip Wasabi is available in both paste and powdered forms. We used the paste, but you can add a few drops of cold water to the powder, as instructed on the label, and use it instead.

Adding tuna, cucumber and avocado

Rolling nori with sushi mat

SPOON FROM TATTI

Chopping lemon grass

Blending pesto ingredients

crisp salmon with lemon-grass pesto

PREPARATION TIME 15 MINUTES • COOKING TIME 7 MINUTES

1/4 cup (35g) roasted unsalted peanuts

2 red Thai chillies, seeded, chopped coarsely

1 stalk fresh lemon grass, chopped coarsely

1/2 cup tightly packed fresh coriander leaves

1/3 cup (80ml) olive oil

1 tablespoon lemon juice

vegetable oil, for shallow-frying

6 salmon cutlets (1kg)

1 Blend or process peanuts, chilli, lemon grass, coriander, olive oil and juice until mixture forms a paste. Cover pesto; refrigerate until required.

2 Heat enough vegetable oil to cover base of large pan; shallow-fry fish both sides, uncovered, until cooked as desired. Drain on absorbent paper.

3 Serve fish topped with pesto.

SERVES 6

per serve 26.6g fat; 1528kJ (excludes oil for shallow-frying)

serving suggestion Serve with baby potatoes tossed in brown butter, and rocket salad with seeded mustard dressing.

sardines with parmesan crumbs and fresh tomato sauce

PREPARATION TIME 12 MINUTES (PLUS REFRIGERATION TIME) • COOKING TIME 30 MINUTES

Butterflied sardines (see page 110) can be used in this recipe.

16 sardine fillets (250g)
¹/₄ cup plain flour (35g)
2 tablespoons milk
1 egg
1 cup stale breadcrumbs (70g)
³/₄ cup coarsely grated parmesan cheese (60g)
vegetable oil, for shallow-frying

FRESH TOMATO SAUCE
1 tablespoon olive oil
1 large brown onion (200g), sliced thinly
2 cloves garlic, crushed
5 medium tomatoes (1kg), seeded, chopped coarsely
2 teaspoons sugar
¹/₃ cup dry white wine (80ml)
2 tablespoons finely shredded fresh basil leaves

1 Coat fish in flour; shake off excess. Dip fish in combined milk and egg; coat in combined breadcrumbs and cheese. Cover; refrigerate 30 minutes.

Coating sardines in breadcrumb mixture

2 Heat oil in large pan; shallow-fry fish, in batches, until browned and just cooked through, drain on absorbent paper. Serve fish with fresh tomato sauce.

fresh tomato sauce Heat the oil in medium pan; cook onion and garlic, stirring, until onion is soft. Add tomato, sugar and wine; simmer, uncovered, about 20 minutes or until sauce has thickened. Stir in basil.

SERVES 4

per serve 16.1g fat; 1448kJ (excludes oil for shallow-frying)
serving suggestion Serve with salad and roasted potato wedges.

Shredding basil

Roasting capsicums

Grilling zucchini slices

bream with antipasto

PREPARATION TIME 25 MINUTES • COOKING TIME 20 MINUTES

You can use any small white fish fillets for this recipe.

2 large red capsicums (700g)
2 large yellow
  capsicums (700g)
4 medium bream
  fillets (800g)
1/3 cup extra virgin
  olive oil (80ml)
11/2 tablespoons
  balsamic vinegar

2 medium zucchini (240g)
200g semi-dried
  tomatoes, chopped
1 medium red onion (170g),
  sliced thinly
2/3 cup kalamata olives
  (100g), seeded
2 tablespoons coarsely
  chopped oregano leaves

1 Quarter capsicums, remove and discard seeds and membranes. Roast under grill or in very hot oven, skin-side up, until skin blisters and blackens. Cover capsicum pieces with plastic or paper for 5 minutes; peel away skin, cut into thick slices.

2 Cover an oven tray with greased foil. Brush fish with combined oil and vinegar; grill about 10 minutes or until lightly browned both sides and cooked through. Cover to keep warm.

3 Meanwhile, cut zucchini lengthways into thin slices. Cook on heated oiled grill plate (or barbecue or grill) until browned both sides.

4 Combine capsicum, zucchini, tomato, onion and olives in large bowl; drizzle with remaining combined oil, vinegar and oregano, toss gently. Serve fish with warm antipasto.

SERVES 4

per serve 25g fat; 1922kJ

paella

PREPARATION TIME 30 MINUTES
COOKING TIME 35 MINUTES

*Paella is a saffron-flavoured rice
combining meat and shellfish,
originating from Spain. It is named
after the two-handled pan in which
it is cooked and served. We used
ling fish fillets in this recipe.*

**6 uncooked large
   prawns (250g)**
250g white fish fillets
1 tablespoon olive oil
**6 green onions,
   chopped coarsely**
**1 large green capsicum
   (350g), chopped coarsely**
**1 large red capsicum (350g),
   chopped coarsely**
**2 cups white long-grain
   rice (400g)**
pinch saffron threads
1 tablespoon tomato paste
1 cup dry white wine (250ml)
**4 medium tomatoes (660g),
   seeded, chopped coarsely**
**3 cups vegetable
   stock (750ml)**
**250g small black mussels,
   prepared (see page 112)**
**250g baby octopus, prepared
   (see page 112)**
200g calamari rings
200g scallops

1 Shell and devein prawns,
  leaving tails intact. Cut fish
  into 3cm pieces.

2 Heat the oil in large pan; cook
  onion and capsicums until
  tender. Add rice; stir to coat in
  oil. Stir in saffron, paste, wine
  and tomato; cook, stirring, until
  wine is absorbed.

3 Add 1 cup (250ml) of the stock;
  cook, stirring, until stock is
  absorbed. Add remaining stock;
  cook, stirring, until mixture
  boils and rice is almost tender.

4 Place all seafood over rice
  mixture; simmer, covered, about
  10 minutes or until seafood
  has just changed colour. Discard
  any mussels that do not open.
  Stand, covered, 5 minutes,
  before serving.

SERVES 6

per serve 6.5g fat; 1961kJ
serving suggestion Start
your Spanish meal with a
selection of tapas.

Removing beards from mussels

Removing octopus beak

salmon and vegetables en croûte

PREPARATION TIME 35 MINUTES • COOKING TIME 30 MINUTES

Croûte literally means "crust". En croûte can refer to food served in a pastry case, or on toasted or fried bread, or, as here, on a piece of puff pastry.

750g piece salmon fillet
1/4 cup lemon juice (60ml)
1 tablespoon olive oil
1 sheet ready-rolled puff pastry
1 egg, beaten lightly
2 medium carrots (240g)
3 trimmed celery sticks (225g)
250g fresh asparagus, trimmed
2/3 cup dry white wine (160ml)
1 cup cream (250ml)
1 tablespoon seeded mustard
1 tablespoon finely chopped fresh chives

Cutting fish into pieces

Cutting diagonal slashes in pastry

1 Remove and discard skin from fish; trim edges and cut fish into 8 slices. Combine fish, juice and the oil in large bowl; cover, refrigerate 3 hours or overnight.

2 Cut pastry into quarters; place on oiled oven tray. Cut shallow diagonal slashes in pastry, at 1cm intervals, to form grid pattern. Brush with egg; bake, uncovered, in moderate oven about 10 minutes or until browned.

3 Meanwhile, cut carrots and celery into matchstick-size pieces. Halve asparagus. Heat oiled large pan; stir-fry vegetables, in batches, until just tender. Cover to keep warm.

4 Drain fish over medium bowl; reserve marinade. Cook fish, in batches, in same pan until browned both sides and cooked as desired. Cover to keep warm.

5 Pour wine and reserved marinade into same pan; bring to boil, simmer, uncovered, until reduced by half. Add cream and mustard; cook, stirring, until sauce thickens slightly, stir through chives.

6 Place pastry pieces on serving plates, top with vegetables, fish and sauce.

SERVES 4

per serve 56g fat; 3457kJ

tip Thaw out only as many sheets of puff pastry as the recipe requires.

sea perch with fattoush

PREPARATION TIME 20 MINUTES • COOKING TIME 15 MINUTES

Fattoush is a Lebanese bread salad. The traditional preparation method is to put the pieces of pitta at the bottom of a salad bowl and moisten them with water. In this recipe, we toss the toasted bread pieces into the fattoush. Other firm, white-fleshed fish fillets can be used instead of sea perch.

2 large pitta bread rounds
2 Lebanese cucumbers (260g)
250g cherry tomatoes, quartered
4 red radishes (140g), chopped coarsely
1 medium green capsicum (200g), chopped coarsely
8 green onions, chopped finely
1/2 cup coarsely chopped fresh flat-leaf parsley

2 tablespoons coarsely chopped fresh mint leaves
1/4 cup olive oil (60ml)
1/4 cup lemon juice (60ml)
1 clove garlic, crushed
1/2 teaspoon ground cumin
1 teaspoon sweet paprika
1 tablespoon vegetable oil
6 sea perch fillets (1.4kg)

1 Place bread on oven trays, grill until browned both sides and crisp. Cool; break into pieces.

2 Halve cucumbers lengthways; using spoon, scoop out seeds, slice cucumber crossways.

3 Combine cucumber, tomato, radish, capsicum, onion, parsley and mint in large bowl; drizzle with combined olive oil, juice, garlic, cumin and paprika, toss gently.

4 Heat vegetable oil in large pan; cook fish both sides, uncovered, until cooked as desired.

5 Toss bread pieces into fattoush; serve with fish.

SERVES 6

per serve 20.4g fat; 2050kJ

Breaking bread into pieces

Seeding and slicing cucumbers

Cutting pide into four "rolls"

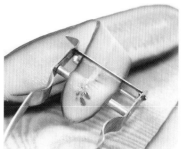
Slicing cucumber into thin strips

fish burgers

PREPARATION TIME 15 MINUTES • COOKING TIME 20 MINUTES

We used shark (also called flake) in this recipe; it has a sweet flavour with a soft texture. Other soft-textured white-fleshed fish can be substituted.

**600g shark fillets,
  chopped coarsely**
1 egg
1/4 teaspoon sweet paprika
1 teaspoon ground cumin
1 teaspoon ground coriander
1/2 teaspoon garlic salt

1 long loaf pide
2 Lebanese cucumbers (260g)
200g yogurt
**1 tablespoon finely chopped
  fresh mint leaves**
**1 tablespoon finely chopped
  preserved lemon**

1 Blend or process fish, egg, paprika, cumin, coriander and garlic salt until smooth; using hands, shape mixture into 4 patties.

2 Cook patties in large heated oiled pan, uncovered, until browned both sides and cooked as desired.

3 Cut pide into 4 even pieces; slice horizontally through the centre of each piece. Toast pieces, cut-side up, under heated grill.

4 Using a vegetable peeler, slice cucumbers into thin strips.

5 Combine remaining ingredients in small bowl.

6 Top pide bases with patties; top with equal amounts of cucumber and yogurt mixture, then remaining pide.

SERVES 4

per serve 8.1g fat; 2205kJ

gravlax with buckwheat blini

PREPARATION TIME 25 MINUTES (PLUS MARINATING AND STANDING TIME) • COOKING TIME 20 MINUTES

Note that the fish in this recipe is uncooked.

**500g salmon fillet,
  with skin on**
**1/4 cup finely chopped
  fresh dill**
1/2 teaspoon sea salt
**1/2 teaspoon cracked
  black pepper**
1/2 teaspoon sugar
1 tablespoon brandy

BUCKWHEAT BLINI

1/2 cup plain flour (75g)
**1/2 cup buckwheat
  flour (75g)**
1/2 teaspoon salt
1 teaspoon dry yeast
2/3 cup hot milk (160ml)
2 eggs, separated
2/3 cup cream (160ml)

HORSERADISH MASCARPONE

250g mascarpone
**1 tablespoon
  horseradish cream**

1 Remove bones from fish
  with tweezers, trim edges
  to neaten if necessary; place
  skin-side down on piece of
  foil. Sprinkle salmon with
  combined dill, salt, pepper
  and sugar, then brandy.
  Wrap salmon in foil, place
  salmon between two trays,
  place weight on top of top
  tray; refrigerate overnight.

2 Finely slice salmon; top a
  buckwheat blini with horseradish
  mascarpone and salmon.
  Repeat with another layer.

buckwheat blini Place sifted
flours, salt and yeast in medium
bowl. Gradually whisk in combined
milk and egg yolks until mixture
is smooth. Cover, stand in warm
place 1 hour or until mixture is
frothy. Beat cream in small bowl
with whisk until soft peaks form,
fold into yeast mixture. Beat egg
whites in small bowl with whisk
until soft peaks form, fold into
yeast mixture. Cover; stand
15 minutes. Pour 2 tablespoons
of batter into heated oiled pan,
cook until browned both sides.
Repeat with remaining batter.

horseradish mascarpone
Combine ingredients in small bowl,
cover, refrigerate until required.

SERVES 6

per serve 37.8g fat; 2126kJ
tips Yeast grows in a warm,
moist environment. To activate
dry yeast, milk should be quite
hot when added.
• Use whisk, rotary beater or
electric mixer for whipping cream
and egg whites. It is important
the bowl be clean and dry for
success in beating egg whites.

Compressing salmon under weighted tray

Sprinkling salmon with dill

Folding cream into yeast mixture

Cooking blini

Drizzling oil over tomato

Cutting radishes into quarters

tuna with salade niçoise

PREPARATION TIME 30 MINUTES (PLUS STANDING TIME)
COOKING TIME 25 MINUTES

Tiny new potatoes are also known as chats. Perfectly shaped vine-ripened tomatoes are ideal to use in this recipe. Salmon steaks can be substituted for tuna.

4 small tomatoes (520g), quartered

2 teaspoons olive oil

500g tiny new potatoes, halved

200g green beans

4 tuna steaks (800g)

4 hard-boiled eggs

300g red radishes, trimmed, quartered

1 large yellow capsicum (350g), seeded, chopped coarsely

100g black olives, seeded

SEEDED MUSTARD DRESSING

5 whole canned anchovy fillets, drained, chopped coarsely

1/4 cup lemon juice (60ml)

1 clove garlic, crushed

1/4 cup grated parmesan cheese (20g)

1/4 cup seeded mustard (60g)

1/2 cup olive oil (125ml)

1 Place tomato in small baking dish, drizzle with the oil; bake, uncovered, in hot oven about 15 minutes or until slightly softened, cool.

2 Meanwhile, boil, steam or microwave potato and beans, separately, until just tender; drain, cool.

3 Cook tuna, in batches, on heated oiled grill plate (or grill or barbecue) until browned both sides and cooked through; cool. Cut tuna into 3.5cm diamonds.

4 Cut each egg into 6 wedges. Combine all ingredients in large bowl; pour over dressing, mix well.

seeded mustard dressing
Blend or process all ingredients until smooth.

SERVES 4

per serve 63.9g fat; 3703kJ

salmon tartare on bruschetta

PREPARATION TIME 20 MINUTES • COOKING TIME 5 MINUTES

Sashimi-quality tuna can be substituted for salmon. Note that the fish in this recipe is uncooked.

200g piece salmon

1 small red onion (100g),
   chopped finely

4 medium tomatoes (760g),
   seeded, chopped finely

1 medium avocado (250g),
   chopped finely

2 tablespoons finely
   chopped fresh dill

1/4 cup extra virgin
   olive oil (60ml)

1 long French bread stick

2 tablespoons olive oil

1 Remove and discard any skin or bones from fish. On clean cutting board, chop fish finely with sharp heavy knife.

2 Place fish in medium bowl with onion, tomato, avocado, dill and extra virgin olive oil; mix gently to combine. Cover; refrigerate briefly while making bruschetta.

3 Cut bread into 1cm slices, brush each slice both sides with olive oil; toast both sides.

4 Spoon tartare mixture onto bruschetta to serve.

SERVES 8

per serve 18g fat; 1095kJ

tip Bruschetta can be made one hour ahead. Cool, then store in airtight container.

Finely dicing salmon

Preparing bruschetta

smoked salmon and rosti stacks

PREPARATION TIME 25 MINUTES • COOKING TIME 15 MINUTES

You can substitute light sour cream for crème fraîche. Russet burbank potatoes are excellent for frying but may be harder to obtain than the kennebecs used in this recipe.

200ml crème fraîche
1 tablespoon finely chopped fresh dill
2 tablespoons horseradish cream
1 teaspoon finely grated lemon rind
5 medium kennebec potatoes (1kg)
1 clove garlic, crushed
1/2 teaspoon cracked black pepper
1/4 cup finely chopped fresh chives
1 egg, beaten lightly
1/4 cup plain flour (35g)
vegetable oil, for shallow-frying
16 thin slices smoked salmon (250g)

1 Combine crème fraîche, dill, horseradish cream and rind in small bowl.

2 Grate potatoes coarsely, squeeze out excess moisture. Combine potato in large bowl with garlic, pepper, chives, egg and flour; mix well.

3 Heat oil in medium pan; cook 1/4 cups of potato mixture, in batches, until browned both sides and crisp. Drain rosti on absorbent paper.

4 Place one rosti on each serving plate, top with two slices salmon and 1 tablespoon crème fraîche mixture; repeat, then finish each stack with a third rosti and remaining crème fraîche mixture.

SERVES 4

per serve 25g fat; 2092kJ (excludes oil for shallow-frying)

Grating potatoes

Squeezing water out of potatoes

lemon-cured sardines

PREPARATION TIME 20 MINUTES (PLUS MARINATING TIME) • COOKING TIME 20 MINUTES

These sardines are not "cooked" in the traditional sense, but are cured by marinating in lemon juice.

**32 uncooked sardine
    fillets (480g)**
¹/₂ cup lemon juice (125ml)
1 large red capsicum (350g)
**4 medium potatoes (800g),
    chopped coarsely**
**1 cup firmly packed fresh
    basil leaves, shredded**

¹/₂ cup pine nuts (80g), toasted
**¹/₃ cup coarsely grated
    parmesan cheese (25g)**
1 clove garlic, quartered
¹/₂ cup olive oil (125ml)
50g baby rocket leaves
**1 small red onion (100g),
    chopped finely**

1 Place fish in single layer
  in shallow dish; pour over
  lemon juice. Cover; refrigerate
  overnight. Drain; discard juice.

2 Quarter capsicum, remove and
  discard seeds and membranes.
  Roast under grill or in very hot
  oven, skin-side up, until skin
  blisters and blackens. Cover
  capsicum pieces with plastic
  or paper for 5 minutes; peel
  away skin and discard. Cut
  flesh into thin slices.

3 Meanwhile, boil, steam
  or microwave potato until
  just tender.

4 Blend or process basil, nuts,
  cheese, garlic and oil until
  smooth. Cover pesto; refrigerate.

5 Just before serving, combine
  fish, capsicum, potato, pesto,
  rocket and onion; toss gently.

SERVES 4

per serve 47.1g fat; 2596kJ
serving suggestion Serve as
a delightful summer appetiser.

Peeling capsicum

Cutting tortillas into triangles

Finely chopping seeded tomatoes

1 Combine chilli powder, salt, oregano, thyme and paprika in small bowl.

2 Brush fish all over with butter; coat with spice mixture.

3 Cook fish, in batches, in heated oiled grill pan (or grill or barbecue) until browned both sides and cooked through. Keep warm.

4 Place garlic in small bowl with the oil; brush oil mixture over both sides of each tortilla. Place tortillas on oven tray; bake, uncovered, in hot oven 5 minutes or until crisp. Cut each tortilla into 8 pieces.

5 Serve fish with tortilla triangles and fresh salsa.

fresh salsa Combine ingredients in small bowl.

SERVES 4

per serve 31.7g fat; 2501kJ

tip You can jazz up your salsa by adding avocado, olives or your favourite vegetable.

cajun orange roughy

PREPARATION TIME 20 MINUTES • COOKING TIME 15 MINUTES

Any firm, white-fleshed fish fillets can be used.

1 teaspoon chilli powder

1 tablespoon garlic salt

2 tablespoons dried oregano

2 tablespoons dried thyme

2 teaspoons sweet paprika

4 orange roughy fillets (1kg)

30g butter, melted

1 clove garlic, crushed

1 tablespoon olive oil

4 corn tortillas

FRESH SALSA

4 medium tomatoes (760g), seeded, chopped finely

1 small red onion (100g), chopped finely

1 tablespoon olive oil

1 tablespoon finely chopped fresh oregano

potato-crusted snapper with curried tomatoes

PREPARATION TIME 30 MINUTES • COOKING TIME 20 MINUTES

You can use any firm-fleshed fish fillets for this recipe.

2 tablespoons peanut oil

1 medium brown onion (150g), chopped finely

1 tablespoon grated fresh ginger

3 cloves garlic, crushed

1 teaspoon garam masala

2 teaspoons ground turmeric

1 teaspoon ground cumin

1 teaspoon ground coriander

4 medium tomatoes (720g), chopped coarsely

4 kaffir lime leaves, torn

2 teaspoons sugar

1/2 cup coconut cream (125ml)

2 tablespoons chopped fresh coriander leaves

4 snapper fillets (800g)

2 small potatoes (240g), sliced thinly

40g butter, melted

1/2 teaspoon ground cumin, extra

1 teaspoon ground turmeric, extra

1 Heat half of the oil in medium pan; cook onion, ginger and two-thirds of the garlic, stirring, until onion is soft. Stir in ground spices; cook, stirring, about 2 minutes or until spices are fragrant. Add tomato, lime leaves and sugar; cook, stirring, about 5 minutes or until tomato is just tender. Pour in cream; simmer, uncovered, stirring occasionally, 10 minutes. Just before serving, discard lime leaves; stir in fresh coriander. *[Can be made 24 hours ahead to this stage. Cover, refrigerate until required.]*

2 Meanwhile heat remaining oil in large pan; cook fish, uncovered, about 5 minutes each side or until just cooked through. Place fish, skin-side down, on oven tray. Place potato in single layer on fish; drizzle with combined butter, extra cumin, extra turmeric and remaining garlic. Cook under heated grill about 10 minutes or until potato is crisp. Serve potato-crusted fish with warm curried tomatoes.

SERVES 4

per serve 30.5g fat; 2231kJ

Adding coconut cream to tomato mixture

Placing potatoes over fish

whiting with spiced chickpeas

PREPARATION TIME 20 MINUTES (PLUS STANDING TIME) • COOKING TIME 20 MINUTES

Whiting is available year-round, and its fine texture makes it suitable for gentle pan-frying. Left whole, whiting is suitable for baking, poaching or grilling. Other small whole fish can be used instead of whiting.

1 teaspoon sweet paprika
1 teaspoon ground cumin
1 clove garlic, crushed
1/4 cup lemon juice (60ml)
4 whole whiting (1.2kg)
1/2 teaspoon ground turmeric
2 teaspoons cumin seeds
1 teaspoon ground coriander
1 tablespoon vegetable oil

2 x 300g cans chickpeas, rinsed, drained
2 red Thai chillies, seeded, chopped finely
2/3 cup vegetable stock (160ml)
3 medium egg tomatoes (225g), peeled, chopped coarsely
2 tablespoons finely shredded fresh coriander leaves

1 Combine paprika, ground cumin, garlic and juice in small bowl. Score one side of each fish; place in large baking dish lined with baking paper, brush with spice mixture.

2 Bake fish, uncovered, in moderate oven about 20 minutes or until cooked through.

3 Meanwhile, heat dry large pan; cook turmeric, cumin seeds and ground coriander, stirring, until fragrant. Add the oil, stir over heat until well combined. Add chickpeas; cook, stirring, until coated with spice mixture. Add chilli and stock; cook, stirring, until hot. Cover to keep warm.

4 Just before serving, stir tomato and fresh coriander into chickpea mixture; serve with fish.

SERVES 4

per serve 9.3g fat; 1397kJ

TILES FROM FRED PAZOTTI; CUTLERY FROM EMPIRE HOMEWARES

Brushing fish with spice mixture

Stirring spices into yogurt mixture

. Tossing whitebait in flour mixture

deep-fried whitebait

PREPARATION TIME 10 MINUTES • COOKING TIME 15 MINUTES

Serve as an entree, or present on a platter as finger food for a party.

20g ghee
1/2 teaspoon ground cumin
1/2 teaspoon ground coriander
200ml yogurt
1 Lebanese cucumber (130g),
  seeded, chopped finely
1 clove garlic, crushed

1 tablespoon lemon juice
1 cup plain flour (150g)
1/4 cup coarsely chopped
  fresh coriander leaves
1 teaspoon garlic salt
500g whitebait
vegetable oil, for deep-frying

1 Heat ghee in small pan; cook cumin and ground coriander, stirring, until fragrant, cool.

2 Combine yogurt, cucumber, garlic and juice in small bowl for dip; stir in spice mixture.

3 Combine flour, fresh coriander and salt in large bowl; add whitebait, in batches, toss until coated.

4 Heat oil in medium pan; deep-fry whitebait, in batches, until browned and cooked through, drain on absorbent paper. Serve with spiced yogurt dip.

SERVES 4

per serve 15g fat; 1566kJ (excludes oil for deep-frying)

48

cioppino

PREPARATION TIME 30 MINUTES (PLUS SOAKING AND FREEZING TIME)
COOKING TIME 45 MINUTES

*Originating in San Francisco's large Italian fishing community, cioppino
is an Italian-American fish stew, somewhat similar to a bouillabaisse.
You can use any firm-fleshed fish instead of swordfish.*

**2 uncooked blue swimmer crabs (700g),
   prepared (see page 113)**
16 large uncooked prawns (500g)
450g swordfish steaks
1 tablespoon olive oil
1 medium brown onion (150g), chopped coarsely
2 trimmed sticks celery (150g), chopped coarsely
3 cloves garlic, crushed
6 medium tomatoes (1kg), chopped coarsely
415g can tomato puree
1/2 cup dry white wine (125ml)
1 1/3 cups fish stock (330ml)
1 teaspoon sugar
200g clams, prepared (see page 112)
200g scallops
2 tablespoons shredded fresh basil leaves
1/3 cup coarsely chopped fresh flat-leaf parsley

1 Chop each crab into pieces with cleaver. Shell and devein prawns, leaving tails intact (see page 111). Chop fish into 2cm pieces.

2 Heat the oil in large pan; cook onion, celery and garlic, stirring, until onion is soft. Add tomato; cook, stirring, 5 minutes or until pulpy. Stir in puree, wine, stock and sugar; simmer, covered, 20 minutes. *[Can be made ahead to this stage. Cover; refrigerate overnight.]*

3 Add crab and clams to pan; simmer, covered, 10 minutes. Discard any clams that do not open. Add prawns, fish and scallops; cook, stirring occasionally, about 5 minutes, or until seafood has changed in colour and is cooked through. Stir in herbs.

SERVES 6

per serve 7.1g fat; 1068kJ
serving suggestion Serve in deep soup bowls with crusty bread.

Chopping crab with cleaver

Chopping swordfish steaks

tuna carpaccio with pesto mash

PREPARATION TIME 30 MINUTES (PLUS FREEZING TIME) • COOKING TIME 25 MINUTES

We used yellowfin (also called ahi) which has a pale pink flesh, with a slightly stronger flavour than that of other tunas. Note that the fish in this recipe is not cooked. The coriander pesto may be made an hour ahead; keep, covered, in refrigerator.

400g piece yellowfin tuna
³/₄ cup tightly packed
fresh coriander leaves
¹/₄ cup pine nuts (40g), toasted
1 clove garlic, quartered
1 tablespoon grated lemon rind
¹/₄ cup grated parmesan
cheese (20g)

¹/₂ cup olive oil (125ml)
3 large potatoes
(900g), quartered
¹/₄ cup milk (60ml)
20g butter
1 tablespoon balsamic vinegar

1 Wrap fish tightly in plastic wrap, freeze about 1 hour or until partly frozen.

2 Cut fish into very thin slices; separate slices with plastic wrap, freeze until required.

3 Blend or process coriander, nuts, garlic, rind and cheese until finely chopped. With motor operating, gradually add half of the oil; process pesto until combined.

4 Boil, steam or microwave potato until tender; drain. Combine potato, milk and butter in medium pan, mash potato mixture over low heat until smooth; stir in pesto.

5 Serve tuna with pesto mash; drizzle with combined remaining oil and vinegar.

SERVES 4

per serve 45.8g fat; 2580kJ

tip Freezing the tuna makes it easy to slice very thinly, and the frozen slices are easy to handle when serving. They thaw quickly.

FORK, PLATES AND DISH FROM EMPIRE HOMEWARES

Separating tuna slices with plastic wrap

silver warehou with asian greens

PREPARATION TIME 15 MINUTES (PLUS STANDING TIME) • COOKING TIME 20 MINUTES

For maximum flavour, leave to marinate overnight. Serve with steamed jasmine rice, if desired.
Other large, firm-fleshed fish fillets can be substituted.

6 silver warehou fillets (1kg)
1/4 teaspoon sesame oil
1/2 cup hoisin sauce (125ml)
2 tablespoons soy sauce
1 teaspoon grated fresh ginger
1 cup plain flour (150g)
vegetable oil, for deep-frying
2 tablespoons sweet
**   chilli sauce**
1/3 cup vegetable stock (80ml)
1 tablespoon peanut oil
300g Chinese cabbage,
**   sliced coarsely**
500g choy sum,
**   chopped coarsely**
500g baby bok choy,
**   chopped coarsely**

1 Combine fish, sesame oil, sauces and ginger in medium bowl; cover, refrigerate 3 hours or overnight.

2 Drain fish over small pan; reserve marinade. Coat fish in flour; shake off excess.

3 Heat vegetable oil in wok or large pan; deep-fry fish, in batches, until browned and crisp, drain on absorbent paper. Cover to keep warm.

4 Bring combined reserved marinade, chilli sauce and stock to boil.

5 Heat peanut oil in clean wok; stir-fry cabbage, choy sum and bok choy until just wilted, stir in marinade mixture. Serve fish with stir-fried vegetables.

SERVES 6

per serve 10.5g fat; 1582kJ (excludes oil for deep-frying)

Deep-frying fish

Chopping vegetables

sauces and dressings

Try these recipes to add a pleasant tang to your favourite seafood

tartare

PREPARATION TIME 10 MINUTES

1 egg yolk
1 tablespoon lemon juice
2 teaspoons Dijon mustard
³/4 cup vegetable oil (180ml)
1/4 cup finely chopped capers (50g)
1/4 cup finely chopped gherkins (45g)
2 tablespoons finely chopped fresh chives
**1 tablespoon finely chopped
    fresh flat-leaf parsley**

Blend or process egg yolk, juice and mustard until smooth. With motor operating, gradually pour in oil; process until thick. Stir in capers, gherkins, chives and parsley.

MAKES 1¹/2 CUPS (375ml)

per tablespoon (20ml) 9.8g fat; 380kJ

thousand island

PREPARATION TIME 5 MINUTES

1/2 cup mayonnaise (125ml)
1/3 cup tomato sauce (80ml)
1/4 teaspoon Tabasco sauce
2 teaspoons Worcestershire sauce
1 teaspoon Dijon mustard

Combine all ingredients in small bowl.

MAKES ³/4 CUP (180ml)

per tablespoon (20ml) 4.3g fat; 258kJ

Left, top to bottom: thousand island dressing; chilli and coriander dipping sauce; tartare sauce; creamy avocado sauce

creamy avocado

PREPARATION TIME 5 MINUTES

1 large avocado (320g)
1/4 cup sour cream (60ml)
1/4 cup mayonnaise (60ml)
2 tablespoons olive oil
1 teaspoon Tabasco sauce
1 clove garlic, quartered
1/4 cup tightly packed fresh coriander leaves
1 tablespoon lemon juice

Blend or process all ingredients until smooth.

MAKES 1¹/2 CUPS (375ml)

per tablespoon (20ml) 6.2g fat; 252kJ

chilli and coriander

PREPARATION TIME 5 MINUTES
COOKING TIME 15 MINUTES

2 large tomatoes (500g), chopped coarsely
1/4 cup water (60ml)
1/3 cup lime juice (80ml)
1/4 cup brown sugar (50g)
1 teaspoon fish sauce
1/3 cup sweet chilli sauce (80ml)
2 tablespoons chopped fresh coriander leaves

Combine tomato, the water, juice, sugar and sauces in medium pan; stir over low heat until sugar dissolves. Bring to boil; simmer, uncovered, about 10 minutes or until sauce thickens. Remove from heat, cool; stir in coriander.

MAKES 1 CUP (250ml)

per tablespoon (20ml) 0.2g fat; 126kJ

TILES FROM COUNTRY FLOORS

Threading marinated fish onto skewers

gemfish kebabs

PREPARATION TIME 20 MINUTES (PLUS MARINATING TIME)
COOKING TIME 50 MINUTES

*You can use any firm white-fleshed fish fillets for this recipe. You need to soak
8 bamboo skewers in water at least 1 hour before using to avoid scorching.*

1/3 cup coarsely chopped
  fresh coriander leaves

2 teaspoons ground cumin

1/4 teaspoon ground turmeric

1 clove garlic, quartered

1 red Thai chilli, seeded,
  chopped coarsely

1 tablespoon peanut oil

1 large red onion (300g),
  sliced thinly

500g gemfish fillets

1kg baby new potatoes, halved

1/4 cup olive oil (60ml)

1 tablespoon cumin seeds, crushed

2 teaspoons sea salt

250g baby spinach leaves

2 teaspoons lemon juice

2 teaspoons white wine vinegar

1 Blend or process 1/4 cup
  of the coriander with cumin,
  turmeric, garlic, chilli, peanut
  oil and a quarter of the onion
  until smooth.

2 Cut fish into 2cm pieces.
  Combine fish with coriander
  mixture in medium bowl, cover;
  refrigerate 3 hours or overnight.

3 Boil, steam or microwave
  potatoes until tender; drain.

4 Toss hot potatoes with
  1 tablespoon of the olive
  oil, cumin seeds, remaining
  onion and salt.

5 Place in single layer in large
  baking dish. Bake, uncovered, in
  moderate oven about 40 minutes
  or until potatoes are browned
  and crisp; place in large bowl.
  Add spinach; toss gently to
  combine with potatoes.

6 Meanwhile, thread fish onto 8
  skewers. Cook kebabs, in batches,
  on heated oiled grill plate (or
  grill or barbecue) until browned
  and cooked through. Combine
  remaining coriander, remaining
  olive oil, juice and vinegar in
  screw-top jar; shake well.

7 Place potato mixture on
  serving plates; top with
  kebabs and dressing.

SERVES 4

per serve 21g fat; 1920kJ

sardines with haloumi and spinach

PREPARATION TIME 15 MINUTES • COOKING TIME 30 MINUTES

**4 large egg tomatoes
(360g), quartered**
1 clove garlic, crushed
2 tablespoons olive oil
12 whole sardines (750g)
200g haloumi, sliced thinly
100g kalamata olives, seeded
100g baby spinach leaves
¹/₃ cup caperberries (55g)
1 clove garlic, crushed, extra
**²/₃ cup olive oil
(160ml), extra**
¹/₄ cup lemon juice (60ml)
1 tablespoon Dijon mustard
**1 tablespoon white
wine vinegar**
**2 tablespoons finely
chopped fresh oregano**

1 Combine tomato, garlic and the oil in large baking dish; bake, uncovered, in hot oven about 20 minutes or until tomato is browned lightly.

2 Cook fish on grill plate (or grill or barbecue) about 5 minutes or until cooked through. Cook haloumi on same grill plate about 2 minutes or until browned.

3 Divide tomato mixture, fish, cheese, olives, spinach and caperberries among serving plates. Combine extra garlic and oil in screw-top jar with juice, mustard, vinegar and oregano; shake well. Drizzle over salad.

SERVES 4

per serve 64.7g fat; 3061kJ

TILES FROM COUNTRY FLOORS

Tomatoes, garlic and oil in baking dish

Cooking haloumi on grill plate

beer-battered fish with chips and tartare sauce

PREPARATION TIME 25 MINUTES (PLUS STANDING TIME) • COOKING TIME 20 MINUTES

This batter crisps brilliantly and can be used with white-fleshed or oily fish fillets, prawns, cuttlefish or squid. Flat or just-opened beer can be used for the batter. To prevent chips becoming soggy, cover the oven tray with absorbent paper.

1¹/₂ cups self-raising flour (225g)

1 egg

1¹/₂ cups beer (375ml)

5 large potatoes (1.5kg), peeled

vegetable oil, for deep-frying

12 medium flathead fillets (660g)

TARTARE SAUCE

1 cup mayonnaise (250ml)

2 teaspoons finely grated lemon rind

1 tablespoon lemon juice

2 tablespoons finely chopped gherkins

2 tablespoons drained capers, chopped finely

1 tablespoon finely chopped fresh dill

1 tablespoon finely chopped fresh chives

1 red jalapeño chilli, seeded, chopped finely

Whisking batter in bowl

1 Whisk flour, egg and beer together in medium bowl until smooth; cover, refrigerate batter 1 hour.

2 Cut potatoes into 1cm-wide slices; cut slices into 1cm-wide strips, dry well. Heat oil in large pan; deep-fry chips, in batches, until browned and cooked through. Place chips on absorbent paper on large oven tray; to keep them hot, place, uncovered, in moderate oven.

Slicing potato into strips

3 Meanwhile, reheat oil. Dip fish in batter; deep-fry in hot oil until browned and crisp.

4 Serve fish and chips with tartare sauce.

tartare sauce Combine ingredients in medium bowl; mix well.

SERVES 4

per serve 25.3g fat; 3670kJ (excludes oil for deep-frying)

serving suggestion Serve with coleslaw.

tip The best potatoes to use for deep-fried chips are Atlantic, Bintje, Nicola, Patrone, Spunta, Russet Burbank and Toolangi Delight.

Dipping fish into batter

Adding filling to the rolls

Rolling and folding rice paper

salmon rice paper rolls

PREPARATION TIME 30 MINUTES

Wasabi is available in both paste and powdered forms. We used the paste but, if you add a few drops of cold water to the powder, as instructed on the label, you can use this mixture as a substitute.

50g rice vermicelli

10 x 22cm-round rice paper sheets

¼ cup crème fraîche (60ml)

2 teaspoons finely chopped
  fresh dill

¼ teaspoon wasabi

2 teaspoons finely grated
  lemon rind

400g thinly sliced
  smoked salmon

4 fresh asparagus spears,
  sliced finely

1 small red onion (100g),
  sliced finely

60g snow pea sprouts

1 Place vermicelli in medium heatproof bowl, cover with boiling water; stand until just tender, drain.

2 Place 1 sheet of rice paper in medium bowl of warm water until just softened; lift from water carefully, place on board.

3 Combine crème fraîche, dill, wasabi and rind in small bowl. Spread 1 teaspoon of crème fraîche mixture in centre of rice paper; top with a slice of salmon and one-tenth of the asparagus, onion, sprouts and vermicelli. Roll to enclose, folding in ends (rolls should be about 8cm long).

4 Repeat with remaining rice paper rounds and filling. To serve, cut each roll in half.

SERVES 4

per serve 4.3g fat; 479kJ

tip Light sour cream can be substituted for crème fraîche.

smoked rainbow trout

PREPARATION TIME 10 MINUTES (PLUS SOAKING TIME) • COOKING TIME 15 MINUTES

Hot smoking is a cooking style in which the flavours of the food are affected by the choice of wood used. Hickory and mesquite are the best-known woods for smoking; however, there are many different varieties available at barbecue and hardware stores. Any whole small fish can be used for this recipe.

350g wood-smoking chips
1/4 cup tightly packed
kaffir lime leaves
3 stalks fresh lemon grass,
chopped coarsely
1 kaffir lime, quartered
2 x 400g rainbow trout

1 Place chips in medium bowl, cover with cold water; stand overnight.

2 Reserve 8 lime leaves and 2 tablespoons lemon grass. Line wok or large pan with foil; place drained chips on foil with remaining leaves, lemon grass and lime. Heat, covered, until smoking.

3 Fill cavity of trout with reserved leaves and lemon grass, place on wire rack over heat; cook, covered, for 20 minutes or until fish is cooked as desired.

SERVES 4

per serve 8.3g fat; 887kJ

tip Wood chips have to be soaked first in cold water so that they will smoulder slowly over the fire rather than burn. For additional flavours and scents, add a variety of herbs and spices to the soaking water. For best results when smoking, try not to interrupt cooking with frequent opening or removal of the lid, as this lessens the intensity of the smoky flavour you're trying to achieve.

PLATE FROM EMPIRE HOMEWARES, TILES FROM COUNTRY FLOORS

Chopping lemon grass coarsely

Placing ingredients in wok

chive and parsley pesto-filled ocean trout

PREPARATION TIME 40 MINUTES • COOKING TIME 20 MINUTES

You will need about 3 bunches of chives (45g) for this recipe. The pesto can be made a day ahead; keep, covered, in refrigerator. Salmon fillets can be used instead of ocean trout.

3/4 cup coarsely chopped fresh chives

1 cup coarsely chopped fresh flat-leaf parsley

1/4 cup pine nuts (40g), toasted

1/2 cup olive oil (125ml)

1 clove garlic, quartered

1/2 cup grated parmesan cheese (40g)

2 large ocean trout fillets (1.2kg), skin left on

200ml crème fraîche

2 tablespoons finely chopped fresh chives, extra

1 Blend or process herbs, nuts, the oil, garlic and cheese until pesto is almost smooth.

2 Place one piece of fish, skin-side down, on board; spread with pesto. Top with remaining fish piece, skin-side up; tie with kitchen string.

3 Place fish in large baking dish; bake, covered, in hot oven 20 minutes. Remove cover, bake about 10 minutes more or until fish is just cooked through.

4 Serve sliced fish with combined crème fraîche and extra chives.

SERVES 6

per serve 42.3g fat; 2050kJ

serving suggestion Serve with creamy mashed potato, if desired.

tip Crème fraîche is available, in cartons, from delicatessens and supermarkets; light sour cream may be used instead.

Spreading pesto over fish

Tying fish with string

molluscs

Oysters, mussels, clams, pipis and scallops... all have a shell as protection for their soft bodies, all have a universe of fans who love them for both their smooth, silky texture and their understated and addictive flavour – a flavour which seems to possess the full, fresh resonance of the sea.

oysters japanese-style

PREPARATION TIME 15 MINUTES

Ketjap manis, also known as kecap manis, is a sweet soy sauce. Wasabi is an Asian horseradish sold in powdered or paste form; either is suitable for this recipe. Nori is a type of dried seaweed, available in paper-thin sheets, toasted or plain; the plain sheets should be lightly toasted in the oven before use.

Chopping pickled ginger

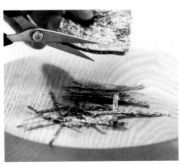

Shredding nori

^{1}/$_4$ **teaspoon wasabi**

2 teaspoons ketjap manis

2 teaspoons rice vinegar

1 tablespoon lime juice

1 tablespoon finely chopped pickled ginger

^{1}/$_4$ **teaspoon sesame oil**

2 tablespoons peanut oil

^{1}/$_2$ **sheet toasted nori**

24 medium oysters on the half shell (1.5kg)

1 tablespoon thinly sliced pickled ginger, extra

1 Whisk wasabi, ketjap manis, vinegar, juice, ginger and oils in small bowl for dressing.

2 Cut nori in half lengthways; shred finely.

3 Arrange oysters on serving plate; drizzle with dressing, sprinkle with nori and extra ginger.

SERVES 4

per serve 12.2g fat; 576kJ

clams with tomato vinaigrette

PREPARATION TIME 30 MINUTES • COOKING TIME 10 MINUTES

2.5kg clams, prepared
  (see page 112)
1/2 cup dry white wine (125ml)
1 small red onion (100g),
  chopped finely
2 cloves garlic, crushed
2 tablespoons lemon juice

2 tablespoons white wine vinegar
1/2 cup olive oil (125ml)
5 large tomatoes (1.25kg),
  chopped coarsely
4 green onions, sliced finely
2 tablespoons coarsely chopped
  fresh coriander leaves

1 Rinse clams under cold water; drain. Place clams in large pan with wine, cover, bring to boil; simmer about 5 minutes or until shells open, discard any that do not open.

2 Meanwhile, heat oiled large pan; cook red onion and garlic over medium heat until lightly browned. Add combined juice, vinegar and oil; cook, stirring, about 2 minutes or until thickened slightly.

3 Drain clams; discard liquid.

4 Gently toss clams with tomato, green onion, coriander and red onion mixture.

SERVES 4

per serve 30.7g fat; 1584kJ
tip Water can be used in place of the white wine, if desired.

Scrubbing clam shells

Stirring in combined juice, vinegar and oil

turmeric scallops with pea puree

PREPARATION TIME 10 MINUTES (PLUS STANDING TIME) • COOKING TIME 20 MINUTES

We used scallops with roe in this recipe; the roe can be discarded, if desired. Most greengrocers stock shelled fresh peas; if not, you will need about 1.2kg of unshelled fresh peas for this recipe, or you can use frozen peas.

32 scallops

**1/3 cup extra virgin
   olive oil (80ml)**

1 clove garlic, crushed

1 teaspoon ground turmeric

PEA PUREE

40g butter

**1 small brown onion (80g),
   chopped finely**

2²/3 cups fresh peas (450g)

**1/4 cup dry white
   wine (60ml)**

1 Combine scallops, the oil, garlic and turmeric in medium bowl; cover, refrigerate 3 hours or overnight.

2 Drain scallops over medium bowl; reserve marinade. Cook scallops, in batches, in heated small pan, uncovered, about 2 minutes each side or until almost cooked through; cover to keep warm. Bring reserved marinade to boil in same pan.

3 Serve scallops with pea puree; drizzle with marinade.

pea puree Heat butter in medium pan; cook onion, stirring, until soft. Stir in peas; cook, stirring, 2 minutes. Add wine, bring to boil; simmer, covered, stirring occasionally, about 10 minutes or until peas are tender. Blend or process pea mixture, in batches, until almost smooth.

SERVES 4

per serve 28g fat; 1467kJ

ORGANZA NAPKIN FROM KINGS, QUEENS & SOUP TUREENS

Cooking scallops

garlic calamari with kumara crisps

PREPARATION TIME 25 MINUTES (PLUS STANDING TIME) • COOKING TIME 20 MINUTES

2 tablespoons lime juice
750g calamari rings
1 teaspoon grated fresh ginger
2 cloves garlic, crushed
vegetable oil, for deep-frying
3 small kumara (750g), sliced thinly
plain flour
1/3 cup fresh coriander leaves

1 Combine juice, calamari, ginger and garlic in large bowl, cover; refrigerate 3 hours or overnight.

2 Heat oil in medium pan; deep-fry kumara, in batches, until crisp. Drain on absorbent paper.

3 Coat calamari in flour; shake away excess. Reheat oil; fry calamari, in batches, until browned and tender, drain on absorbent paper. Serve calamari with kumara crisps, coriander, and lime wedges if desired.

SERVES 4

per serve 3g fat; 1678kJ (excludes oil for deep-frying)

tip Crisps and calamari can be cooked in a wok, deep-fryer, heavy-base saucepan or deep frying pan; the oil should be about 4cm deep.

Frying kumara

Coating calamari in flour

couscous-topped mussels

PREPARATION TIME 30 MINUTES • COOKING TIME 15 MINUTES

Other types of mussels may be used in place of the greenlip mussels, if preferred.

¹/₂ cup couscous (100g)

¹/₂ cup boiling water (125ml)

20g butter

1 tablespoon finely shredded
   fresh mint leaves

1 clove garlic, crushed

2 teaspoons ground cumin

1 teaspoon sweet paprika

¹/₄ teaspoon chilli powder

1 small tomato (130g), seeded,
   chopped finely

1 tablespoon pine nuts, toasted,
   chopped finely

2 green onions, chopped finely

2 tablespoons finely
   chopped dried dates

1 tablespoon olive oil

2 tablespoons finely grated
   lemon rind

1 tablespoon lemon juice

¹/₃ cup tightly packed fresh
   coriander leaves, chopped

24 greenlip mussels (700g),
   prepared (see page 112)

1 Combine couscous with the
   water in medium heatproof
   bowl, cover, stand about
   5 minutes or until water is
   absorbed; fluff with a fork.

2 Heat butter in medium pan; stir
   in couscous. Add mint, garlic,
   spices, tomato, nuts, onion,
   dates, the oil, half the rind,
   juice and half the coriander;
   toss with a fork to combine.

3 Boil, steam or microwave
   mussels until shells open,
   discard any that do not.
   Break open shells; discard
   tops. Loosen mussels from
   bottom shells with a spoon.

4 Serve mussels in bottom shells,
   topped with warm couscous and
   sprinkled with remaining rind
   and coriander.

SERVES 4

per serve 14.2g fat; 1116kJ

serving suggestion Serve
mussels on a large platter
with wedges of lime.

Loosening mussels from shells

ORANGE ORGANZA NAPKIN FROM KINGS, QUEENS & SOUP TUREENS

Crushing peppercorns

Adding cooked scallops

sichuan scallops

PREPARATION TIME 20 MINUTES (PLUS STANDING TIME)
COOKING TIME 10 MINUTES

We removed the roe from the scallops but, if you prefer, they can be left intact.

32 scallops
1 tablespoon Sichuan
  peppercorns, crushed
1 tablespoon peanut oil
1 medium red onion (170g),
  sliced thinly
1 clove garlic, crushed
2 teaspoons grated fresh ginger

1 medium red capsicum (200g),
  sliced thinly
1 medium yellow capsicum (200g),
  sliced thinly
500g spinach, trimmed
1/3 cup oyster sauce (80ml)
2 tablespoons rice vinegar

1 Combine scallops with peppercorns in medium bowl; cover, refrigerate 3 hours or overnight.

2 Heat oil in wok or large pan; stir-fry scallops, in batches, until scallops are changed in colour and cooked through.

3 Stir-fry onion, garlic, ginger and capsicums in same wok until vegetables are almost tender. Add spinach, sauce and vinegar; stir-fry until spinach just wilts. Add scallops, stir-fry until hot.

SERVES 4

per serve 6.4g fat; 780kJ
serving suggestion Sichuan scallops can be served with fresh rice noodles.

oysters

Here are recipes for three classic ways of serving oysters. A fourth, Oysters Natural, is even simpler. Serve oysters on the half shell with lemon wedges, slices of buttered brown bread and bottled cocktail sauce, or you can make your own (see page 93).

oysters kilpatrick

PREPARATION TIME 5 MINUTES
COOKING TIME 10 MINUTES

**24 medium oysters on the
half shell (1.5kg)**
**4 bacon rashers (280g),
chopped finely**
**2 tablespoons
Worcestershire sauce**

Place oysters on oven tray; top with bacon, drizzle with sauce. Grill until bacon is crisp.

SERVES 4

per serve 14g fat; 1296kJ

oysters rockefeller

PREPARATION TIME 10 MINUTES
COOKING TIME 10 MINUTES

80g butter
2 cloves garlic, crushed
**500g spinach, trimmed,
chopped coarsely**
**24 medium oysters on the
half shell (1.5kg)**
**1/3 cup stale
breadcrumbs (25g)**

Melt half the butter in medium pan. Add garlic and spinach; cook, stirring, about 3 minutes or until spinach is wilted. Place oysters on oven tray; top with spinach mixture, sprinkle with breadcrumbs, drizzle with remaining melted butter. Grill until breadcrumbs are golden brown.

SERVES 4

per serve 21g fat; 1270kJ

oysters mornay

PREPARATION TIME 5 MINUTES
COOKING TIME 20 MINUTES

60g butter
1/3 cup plain flour (50g)
2 cups milk (500ml)
**1/2 cup coarsely grated
cheddar cheese (60g)**
**24 medium oysters on the
half shell (1.5kg)**

Melt butter in medium pan, add flour; cook, stirring, about 3 minutes or until mixture thickens and bubbles. Remove from heat, gradually stir in milk; cook, stirring, until mixture boils and thickens. Remove from heat, stir in half the cheese. Place oysters on oven tray; spoon sauce onto oysters, sprinkle with remaining cheese. Grill until browned lightly.

SERVES 4

per serve 26g fat; 1762kJ

opposite: oysters kilpatrick (*left*);
oysters rockefeller (*centre*);
oysters mornay (*right*)

Quartering octopus

Reducing wine mixture

slow-simmered octopus

PREPARATION TIME 20 MINUTES • COOKING TIME 1 HOUR 45 MINUTES

This slow-simmered dish tastes even better if it is cooked a day ahead to allow the flavours to develop. Keep, covered, in refrigerator; reheat before serving.

1kg baby octopus, prepared (see page 112)
1 tablespoon olive oil
1 large brown onion (200g), chopped coarsely
3 cloves garlic, crushed
1 cup dry red wine (250ml)

2 x 400g cans tomatoes
6 canned anchovy fillets, chopped coarsely
1/4 cup tomato paste (60g)
1/4 cup coarsely chopped fresh oregano

1 Quarter each octopus.

2 Heat oil in large pan; cook onion and garlic, stirring, until onion is soft.

3 Add octopus; cook, stirring, until just changed in colour.

4 Add wine; cook, stirring, about 5 minutes or until liquid is reduced by about one-third.

5 Add undrained crushed tomatoes and remaining ingredients; simmer, uncovered, about 1 1/2 hours or until octopus is tender.

SERVES 4

per serve 8.5g fat; 1454kJ
serving suggestion Serve with steamed rice and a green salad.

squid and crisp prosciutto

PREPARATION TIME 15 MINUTES • COOKING TIME 15 MINUTES

You can substitute cuttlefish for the squid hoods, if desired.

1kg squid hoods
2 egg whites
1 teaspoon sea salt
1 teaspoon cracked
   black pepper
vegetable oil, for deep-frying

CRISP PROSCIUTTO

120g thinly sliced prosciutto
2 tablespoons brown sugar
1 tablespoon warm water

GARLIC MAYONNAISE

2 egg yolks
2 teaspoons lemon juice
2 cloves garlic, crushed
³/₄ cup olive oil (180ml)

1 Cut squid in half lengthways; score inside surface of each piece, cut into 2cm-wide strips.

2 Whisk egg whites, salt and pepper in small bowl.

3 Heat oil in wok or large pan. Dip squid in egg mixture; deep-fry, in batches, until squid is tender, drain on absorbent paper.

4 Serve squid with crisp prosciutto and garlic mayonnaise.

crisp prosciutto Dip each prosciutto slice in combined sugar and water; fold in half lengthways, twist into rosette shape. Place on oiled oven tray; bake in hot oven about 10 minutes or until browned and crisp.

garlic mayonnaise Blend or process yolks, juice and garlic until smooth. With motor operating, gradually add the oil in thin stream; process until mayonnaise thickens. Transfer to small bowl; cover, refrigerate until required.

SERVES 4

per serve 50.4g fat; 2867kJ (excludes oil for deep-frying)

tip If mayonnaise is too thick, stir in a teaspoon or two of warm water to thin.

Twisting prosciutto into rosettes

vodka mussels with lemon dill risotto

PREPARATION TIME 15 MINUTES • COOKING TIME 45 MINUTES

2 tablespoons olive oil
2 small brown onions (160g), chopped finely
1¹/₂ cups arborio rice (300g)
1 litre hot vegetable stock (4 cups)
2 cloves garlic, crushed
2 red Thai chillies, chopped finely
¹/₃ cup coarsely chopped fresh parsley stems
¹/₃ cup vodka (80ml)
24 medium black mussels (600g), prepared (see page 112)
2 tablespoons finely grated lemon rind
2 tablespoons finely chopped fresh dill

1 Heat half of the oil in large pan; cook half of the onion, stirring, until soft. Add rice; stir to coat in oil mixture. Stir in 1 cup stock; cook, stirring, over low heat until liquid is absorbed. Continue adding stock in 1-cup batches, stirring until absorbed before next addition. Total cooking time should be about 35 minutes or until rice is just tender.

2 Meanwhile, heat remaining oil in medium pan; cook remaining onion, garlic and chilli, stirring, until onion is soft. Stir in parsley and vodka; cook, stirring, 2 minutes. Stir in mussels; cook, covered, about 10 minutes or until mussels open. Discard any that do not open.

3 Drain mussels over medium heatproof bowl; reserve liquid. Pick out mussels, shake off cooking solids, place mussels in medium bowl. Stir reserved liquid into risotto; cook risotto, stirring, until liquid is absorbed.

4 Stir rind and dill into risotto; serve with mussels.

SERVES 4

per serve 14g fat; 1848kJ

tip If arborio rice is unavailable, some other types of short- or medium-grain rice are suitable for risotto.

Chopping parsley stems

Shaking cooking solids off mussels

calamari rings with chermoulla

PREPARATION TIME 20 MINUTES • COOKING TIME 15 MINUTES

Chermoulla, a classic Moroccan seasoning, is best made several hours ahead; keep, covered, in refrigerator.

1¹/₂ teaspoons chilli powder
3 teaspoons garlic salt
¹/₂ cup plain flour (75g)
1kg calamari rings
vegetable oil, for shallow-frying

CHERMOULLA

¹/₂ teaspoon hot paprika
1 red Thai chilli, seeded,
  chopped finely

1 small red onion (100g),
  chopped finely
1 tablespoon finely grated
  lemon rind
2 cloves garlic, crushed
¹/₄ cup lemon juice (60ml)
¹/₃ cup olive oil (80ml)
¹/₂ cup finely chopped fresh
  flat-leaf parsley

1 Combine chilli powder, salt and flour in small bowl. Coat calamari in flour mixture; shake away excess.

2 Heat oil in medium pan; cook calamari, in batches, until browned and tender, drain on absorbent paper. Serve calamari with chermoulla.

chermoulla Combine all ingredients in small bowl.

SERVES 4

per serve 22.7g fat; 1952kJ (excludes oil for shallow-frying)

Frying calamari

Combining chermoulla ingredients

char-grilled baby octopus salad

PREPARATION TIME 20 MINUTES (PLUS STANDING TIME) • COOKING TIME 15 MINUTES

We used a bottled, commercially made pesto, flavoured with roasted capsicums, for this recipe.

**1.5kg baby octopus,
    prepared (see page 112)**
1 lemon
4 cloves garlic, crushed
1 teaspoon hot paprika
1 teaspoon ground cumin
2 tablespoons pesto
**1/4 cup balsamic
    vinegar (60ml)**
1/2 cup olive oil (125ml)
2 medium tomatoes (380g)
250g baby rocket, trimmed
**100g baby spinach
    leaves, trimmed**
**1 medium red onion (170g),
    sliced thinly**
**100g fetta cheese,
    chopped coarsely**
100g black olives, seeded
2 tablespoons lemon juice

1 Cut each octopus in half.

2 Using vegetable peeler, remove five wide strips of rind from lemon; shred strips finely.

3 Combine octopus, rind, garlic, paprika, cumin, pesto, vinegar and half of the oil in large bowl; cover, refrigerate 3 hours or overnight.

4 Drain octopus over small pan; reserve marinade. Cook octopus, in batches, on heated oiled grill plate (or grill or barbecue) until tender; place in large heatproof serving bowl, cover to keep warm.

5 Bring marinade to boil; pour over octopus.

6 Cut tomatoes into thin wedges; add to octopus with rocket, spinach, onion, cheese and olives, mix gently.

7 Combine juice with remaining oil in small jug; drizzle over octopus salad.

SERVES 4

per serve 47.3g fat; 3185kJ

Peeling rind from lemon

new england clam chowder

PREPARATION TIME 35 MINUTES (PLUS STANDING TIME) • COOKING TIME 20 MINUTES

Pipis may be substituted for the clams, if desired; prepare as for clams. Another version, Manhattan Clam Chowder, uses canned tomatoes, rather than the cream sauce, for its base.

Draining clams

Cooking vegetables and bacon

Stirring flour into butter

1.5kg clams, prepared (see page 112)
1 cup dry white wine (250ml)
1.5 litres water (6 cups)
1 small brown onion (80g), chopped finely
1 small carrot (70g), chopped finely
1/2 small red capsicum (75g), chopped finely
1 trimmed celery stick (75g), chopped finely
2 cloves garlic, crushed
2 bacon rashers (140g), chopped finely
90g butter
2/3 cup plain flour (100g)
130g can corn kernels, drained
300ml cream
1 loaf sourdough
2 tablespoons olive oil
1 tablespoon shredded fresh basil leaves

1 Drain clams, place in large pan with wine, cover, bring to boil; simmer about 3 minutes or until shells open, discard any that do not. Drain clams over medium heatproof bowl; reserve liquid. Remove meat from clams; discard shells. Strain reserved liquid into clean large bowl; discard any residue that has settled in heatproof bowl. Add the water to liquid in bowl.

2 Combine onion, carrot, capsicum, celery, garlic and bacon in large pan; cook, stirring, about 3 minutes or until vegetables soften slightly. Remove from pan; reserve.

3 Heat butter in same large pan; cook flour, stirring, about 3 minutes or until mixture thickens and bubbles. Gradually stir in reserved liquid; stir until mixture boils and thickens. Add clams, corn, cream and reserved vegetable mixture; cook, stirring, about 3 minutes or until hot.

4 Meanwhile, cut sourdough to give twelve 1cm-thick slices; use remaining bread for another use. Brush both sides of slices with oil. Toast bread, in batches, on heated grill plate (or grill or barbecue) until browned both sides.

5 Stir basil through chowder; serve with toast.

SERVES 6

per serve 66.4g fat; 4384kJ

Draining oysters

TILES FROM COUNTRY FLOORS

lemon basil oysters

PREPARATION TIME 25 MINUTES • COOKING TIME 20 MINUTES

We used Pacific oysters for this recipe, but other types of oysters are also suitable. Capsicum tapenade can be made a day ahead; keep, covered, in refrigerator.

1/2 cup cornflour (75g)
1/4 cup iced water (60ml)
1 tablespoon finely grated
  lemon rind
2 tablespoons finely shredded
  fresh basil leaves
1 egg yolk
20 medium oysters on the
  half shell (1.25kg)
vegetable oil, for deep-frying

CAPSICUM TAPENADE
1 small red capsicum (150g)
1 teaspoon drained capers
1 clove garlic, chopped
1 tablespoon olive oil

1 Blend cornflour with the water in medium bowl; whisk in rind, basil and yolk, whisk until batter is smooth.

2 Remove oysters from shells; reserve shells. Drain oysters on absorbent paper. Wash reserved shells; place on oven tray, heat in moderate oven 10 minutes.

3 Meanwhile, heat oil in medium pan. Dip oysters in batter, deep-fry oysters, in batches, until browned; drain on absorbent paper.

4 Serve oysters in shells, topped with capsicum tapenade.

capsicum tapenade Quarter capsicum, remove and discard seeds and membranes. Roast under grill or in very hot oven, skin-side up, until skin blisters and blackens. Cover capsicum pieces with plastic or paper for 5 minutes, peel away skin. Blend or process capsicum with remaining ingredients until almost smooth.

SERVES 4

per serve 8.8g fat; 883kJ
(excludes oil for deep-frying)

cream of mussel soup

PREPARATION TIME 15 MINUTES • COOKING TIME 30 MINUTES

40 small black mussels (1kg),
   prepared (see page 112)
1 cup dry white wine (250ml)
60g butter
8 green onions, chopped finely
1/2 teaspoon curry powder
1/4 cup plain flour (35g)

1 cup vegetable stock (250ml)
2 cups water (500ml)
1 tablespoon tomato paste
3/4 cup cream (180ml)
1 tablespoon finely chopped
   fresh dill

1 Combine mussels and wine in large pan, cover, bring to boil; simmer, covered, about 5 minutes or until mussels open. Discard any unopened mussels. Drain mussels over medium heatproof bowl; reserve liquid.

2 Heat butter in large pan; cook onion and curry powder until onion is soft. Add flour; cook, stirring, about 2 minutes or until mixture thickens and bubbles. Gradually stir in reserved liquid, stock, the water and paste; stir until mixture boils and thickens.

3 Return mussels to pan with cream and dill; simmer, stirring, until heated through.

SERVES 4

per serve 33.1g fat; 1831kJ
serving suggestion Serve with crunchy toasted Turkish bread.

tip Remove flour mixture from heat when adding liquid, to stop lumps forming.

Draining opened mussels over bowl

char-grilled squid with watercress salad

PREPARATION TIME 20 MINUTES (PLUS STANDING TIME)
COOKING TIME 10 MINUTES

Baby octopus may be used in place of the squid, if desired.

1kg squid hoods
1¹/₂ teaspoons ground cumin
2 tablespoons finely chopped fresh dill
2 tablespoons lemon juice
2 tablespoons barbecue sauce
¹/₄ cup sweet chilli sauce (60ml)
¹/₄ cup peanut oil (60ml)
1 tablespoon finely grated lemon rind
2 cloves garlic, crushed
2 Lebanese cucumbers (260g)
1 medium red capsicum (200g), sliced thinly
140g watercress
1 tablespoon water

1 Cut squid in half lengthways; score inside surface of each piece diagonally into 2cm-wide strips.

2 Combine cumin, dill, juice, sauces and the oil in small jug; mix well.

3 Combine squid, rind and garlic in large bowl with half of the cumin mixture; cover, refrigerate 3 hours or overnight. Cover remaining cumin mixture; refrigerate until required.

4 Drain squid; discard marinade. Cook squid, in batches, in heated oiled grill pan (or grill or barbecue) until tender and browned all over; cover to keep warm.

5 Halve cucumbers lengthways; cut into thin slices. Combine cucumber with capsicum and watercress in large bowl.

6 Stir the water into reserved cumin mixture; pour over salad, toss gently to combine. Serve squid with salad.

SERVES 4

per serve 18.3g fat; 1648kJ

Chopping dill

Char-grilling squid

cuttlefish satay salad

PREPARATION TIME 35 MINUTES (PLUS STANDING TIME) • COOKING TIME 15 MINUTES

For extra "heat", sprinkle finely chopped red or green Thai chillies over the salad.

**1.25kg cuttlefish, prepared
(see page 113)**

2 teaspoons ground cumin

2 teaspoons ground coriander

4 cloves garlic, crushed

**2 tablespoons coarsely
chopped fresh lemon grass**

**6 fresh kaffir lime leaves,
shredded finely**

2 tablespoons peanut oil

2 tablespoons lime juice

**1/4 cup crunchy peanut
butter (65g)**

1/3 cup coconut milk (80ml)

**1 tablespoon sweet
chilli sauce**

**2 tablespoons lime
juice, extra**

1 teaspoon brown sugar

**vegetable oil, for
shallow-frying**

**1 small red onion (100g),
sliced thinly**

125g bean sprouts

**1 small Chinese cabbage
(400g), shredded coarsely**

**1/2 cup roasted unsalted
peanuts (75g), chopped**

1 Cut cuttlefish hoods and
tentacles in half lengthways.
Score inside surface of hood
pieces. Combine hoods,
tentacles, spices, garlic, lemon
grass, leaves, peanut oil and
juice in large bowl; cover,
refrigerate 3 hours or overnight.

2 Drain cuttlefish;
discard marinade.

3 Whisk combined peanut butter,
milk, sauce, extra juice and
sugar in small bowl until
satay dressing is smooth.

4 Heat vegetable oil in large
pan; shallow-fry cuttlefish,
in batches, until tender,
drain on absorbent paper.

5 Combine warm cuttlefish,
onion, sprouts, cabbage and
peanuts in large bowl; drizzle
with satay dressing.

SERVES 4

per serve 29.3g fat; 1089kJ
(excludes oil for shallow-frying)

Scoring cuttlefish hoods

pipis stir-fried in coconut milk

PREPARATION TIME 15 MINUTES (PLUS STANDING TIME) • COOKING TIME 10 MINUTES

Clams or mussels may be used in place of the pipis.

TILES FROM COUNTRY FLOORS

Sprinkling pipis with salt

Chopping choy sum

1 tablespoon peanut oil

1 medium brown onion (150g),
  chopped coarsely

1 tablespoon grated fresh ginger

2 cloves garlic, crushed

1 tablespoon finely chopped
  fresh lemon grass

2 teaspoons ground cumin

2 teaspoons ground coriander

1 teaspoon ground turmeric

1kg pipis, prepared
  (see page 112)

2 tablespoons lime juice

2 teaspoons fish sauce

400ml coconut milk

2 teaspoons brown sugar

500g choy sum, chopped coarsely

2 tablespoons fresh
  coriander leaves

1 Heat the oil in wok or large
   pan, add onion, ginger, garlic,
   lemon grass and ground spices;
   stir-fry until fragrant.

2 Add rinsed and drained pipis,
   juice, sauce, milk and sugar;
   stir-fry until pipis open, discard
   any that do not open.

3 Add choy sum; stir-fry until
   leaves are just wilted. Serve
   sprinkled with fresh coriander.

SERVES 4

per serve 9.6g fat; 643kJ

crustaceans

While the name serves to classify these as invertebrates having jointed legs, it does little to convey the singularly luscious quality and delightfully subtle taste of some of our favourite shellfish... we leave that to the way we prepare the prawns, crabs, scampi, lobster and yabbies in this chapter.

chilli crab

PREPARATION TIME 20 MINUTES • COOKING TIME 20 MINUTES

You can substitute prawns for the crab in this recipe, if desired. Palm sugar can be bought in two forms: either in a hard, rock-like block, which pieces can be chipped off, or in a thick syrup that can be measured with a spoon. Both types are available from specialty stores and Asian supermarkets.

4 medium uncooked blue swimmer crabs (3kg)

1 tablespoon peanut oil

2 red Thai chillies, seeded, chopped finely

1 tablespoon grated fresh ginger

2 cloves garlic, crushed

2 teaspoons fish sauce

25g palm sugar, chopped finely

1/4 cup lime juice (60ml)

1/4 cup rice vinegar (60ml)

1/4 cup fish stock (60ml)

3 green onions, sliced thickly

1/4 cup tightly packed fresh coriander leaves

Chopping crab into quarters

1 Prepare crab, leaving flesh in claws and legs (see page 113). Chop each crab body into quarters with cleaver or strong sharp knife.

2 Heat the oil in wok or large pan; cook chilli, ginger, garlic, sauce, sugar, juice, vinegar and stock, stirring, until sugar has dissolved.

3 Add crab; cook, covered, about 15 minutes or until crab has changed in colour. Stir in onion and coriander.

SERVES 4

per serve 6.1g fat; 806kJ

serving suggestion Serve with crusty bread, and provide finger bowls of lemon water and large serviettes.

tip Use shell crackers (like nut crackers) to make eating the crab easier.

Chopping chillies

Combining prawn mixture

Cooking prawns in batches

garlic prawns

PREPARATION TIME 15 MINUTES • COOKING TIME 10 MINUTES

Prawns must be cooked just before serving.

24 large uncooked prawns (1kg)
¼ cup olive oil (60ml)
6 cloves garlic, crushed
2 red Thai chillies, chopped finely
2 teaspoons sea salt flakes
1 tablespoon finely chopped
   fresh flat-leaf parsley

1 Shell and devein prawns, leaving tails intact (see page 111). Combine prawns with 2 tablespoons of the oil, garlic, chilli, salt and parsley in large bowl.

2 Heat remaining oil in large pan; cook prawn mixture, in batches, stirring over high heat until prawns are just changed in colour.

SERVES 4

per serve 15.1g fat, 1010kJ

serving suggestion Serve with baked kipfler potatoes, or kumara chips and mixed salad leaves.

angel hair pasta with scampi

PREPARATION TIME 30 MINUTES • COOKING TIME 30 MINUTES

We used bottled roast capsicum pesto in this recipe, but you can use whichever flavour pesto you prefer.

1 tablespoon olive oil
2 large brown onions (400g),
    chopped finely
4 cloves garlic, crushed
2 x 400g cans tomatoes
2 tablespoons roasted
    capsicum pesto
1 teaspoon sugar

1/2 cup dry white wine (125ml)
375g angel hair pasta
24 uncooked scampi (1.2kg),
    prepared (see page 111)
1/2 cup tightly packed fresh
    basil leaves, shredded

1 Heat oil in large pan; cook onion and garlic until onion is just browned.

2 Add undrained crushed tomatoes, pesto, sugar and wine; simmer, uncovered, about 15 minutes or until sauce thickens slightly.

3 Meanwhile, cook pasta in large pan of boiling water until just tender; drain.

4 Add scampi flesh to tomato mixture; simmer, uncovered, until just changed in colour. Stir in basil.

5 Serve sauce over pasta.

SERVES 4

per serve 10.3g fat; 2565kJ
serving suggestion Can be served as an entree or as a main meal with lots of crusty bread and green salad.

Removing scampi flesh from shells

balmain bug laksa

PREPARATION TIME 45 MINUTES • COOKING TIME 30 MINUTES

In Asia, seafood was traditionally cheaper than meat, and the laksa –
a seafood curry ladled onto noodles – is testament to this.

1 small leek (200g)
vegetable oil, for shallow-frying
16 large uncooked prawns (630g)
3 cups water (750ml)
8 medium cooked Balmain bugs (1kg), prepared (see page 111)
1 tablespoon peanut oil
3/4 cup laksa paste (210g)
3 cups coconut milk (750ml)
8 kaffir lime leaves
2 teaspoons fish sauce
200g thin fresh egg noodles
1 small red capsicum (150g), sliced thinly
100g bean sprouts
50g snow peas, sliced thinly
4 green onions, chopped finely
1/3 cup loosely packed fresh coriander leaves
1/4 cup chopped cashews (35g), roasted

Cutting leek into thin strips

1 Halve leek lengthways; discard roots and green stem, cut white section into thin strips. Shallow-fry leek in vegetable oil, in batches, until browned lightly; drain on absorbent paper.

2 Shell and devein prawns, leaving tails intact (see page 111).

3 Place the water in large pan, cover, bring to boil. Add seafood; simmer, uncovered, about 2 minutes or until just cooked. Drain seafood over large bowl; reserve stock.

Draining seafood

4 Heat peanut oil in large pan; cook paste, stirring, 2 minutes. Add milk, lime leaves and reserved stock; simmer, uncovered, 15 minutes. Stir in sauce and seafood; simmer about 2 minutes or until heated through.

5 Meanwhile, place noodles in large heatproof bowl, cover with boiling water, stand until just tender; drain. Divide noodles among serving bowls; add capsicum, sprouts, peas and seafood mixture. Top with leek, onion, coriander and nuts.

SERVES 4

per serve 58.1g fat; 3660kJ (excludes oil for shallow-frying)

Adding milk and leaves

tomato chilli prawns

PREPARATION TIME 25 MINUTES • COOKING TIME 15 MINUTES

**24 large uncooked
prawns (1kg)**
1/4 cup olive oil (60ml)
**1 medium brown onion
(150g), chopped finely**
1 clove garlic, crushed
**3 large tomatoes (750g),
seeded, chopped finely**
**2 red Thai chillies,
chopped finely**

1 Shell and devein prawns, leaving
tails intact (see page 111). Heat
1 tablespoon of the oil in large
pan; cook prawns, in batches,
until just changed in colour.

2 Heat half of the remaining oil
in medium saucepan; cook
onion and garlic, stirring,
until onion is soft. Add tomato
and chilli; cook, stirring, until
tomato begins to soften.

3 Return prawns to large pan with
tomato mixture; cook, stirring,
until heated through. Stir
through the remaining oil.

SERVES 4

per serve 15.1g fat; 1075kJ
serving suggestion Serve with
wilted spinach leaves as an entree,
or stirred through cooked pasta.

Combining prawns and tomato mixture

prawn cocktail

PREPARATION TIME 45 MINUTES

Note that the cocktail sauce contains uncooked egg yolks (see page 114).

**36 medium cooked
prawns (900g)**
**1 medium iceberg
lettuce, shredded**

COCKTAIL SAUCE
2 egg yolks
1 tablespoon white vinegar
1 tablespoon Dijon mustard
1 cup olive oil (250ml)
1 teaspoon Tabasco sauce
**1 tablespoon
Worcestershire sauce**
1/4 cup tomato sauce (60ml)
2 teaspoons lemon juice

1 Shell and devein prawns,
leaving heads and tails
intact (see page 111).

2 Just before serving, divide
prawns and lettuce among
serving plates; drizzle
with sauce.

cocktail sauce Blend or
process yolks, vinegar and
mustard until smooth; with
motor operating, add oil in
thin stream, process until
mayonnaise thickens. Transfer
to medium bowl; stir in
combined sauces and juice.

SERVES 6

per serve 42g fat; 2000kJ

serving suggestion Perfect
as a first course for a lazy
Sunday lunch, followed by
a barbecued steak.

tip You can also serve the
dressing as a dipping sauce for
pan-fried fish fillets or oysters.

Shelling prawns

Making cocktail sauce

lobster with burnt lemon butter

PREPARATION TIME 40 MINUTES (PLUS FREEZING TIME)
COOKING TIME 20 MINUTES

4 small live lobsters (2.4kg)
1 medium lemon (140g)
150g butter
2 tablespoons finely chopped fresh flat-leaf parsley

1 Place lobsters in freezer for 2 hours; this is the most humane way of killing them. Prepare as for cooked lobster (see page 111), removing and discarding head, halving tail lengthways and leaving flesh in shell.

2 Place lobster in large baking dish, cut-side up; cook, uncovered, in hot oven about 15 minutes or until lobster is just changed in colour and flesh is tender. Cut each lobster half into two pieces, if desired, before serving.

3 Peel rind from lemon; cut into thin slices (you need 2 tablespoons thinly sliced rind). Juice lemon (you need 2 tablespoons of juice).

4 Heat butter and juice in medium pan; cook, stirring, until butter is golden brown, remove from heat, pour over lobster. Sprinkle with parsley and rind.

SERVES 4

per serve 45.4g fat; 3613kJ

serving suggestion Serve lobster with baked winter root vegetables.

tip You could use frozen uncooked lobster tails, if you prefer.

Thinly slicing rind

Browning butter

tamarind yabbies with pakoras

PREPARATION TIME 50 MINUTES (PLUS STANDING TIME) • COOKING TIME 30 MINUTES

Chickpea flour – also known as garam flour or besan – is made from ground chickpeas and is used to make Indian bread and pakoras.

1 tablespoon peanut oil

1 medium brown onion (150g),
 sliced thinly

1 tablespoon grated fresh ginger

2 cloves garlic, crushed

1 tablespoon thick
 tamarind concentrate

1 tablespoon lime juice

1 tablespoon brown sugar

1/3 cup water (80ml)

4 medium tomatoes (760g),
 chopped coarsely

24 medium uncooked yabbies
 (1.5kg), prepared (see page 111)

50g baby spinach leaves

PAKORAS

1/2 cup self-raising flour (75g)

1/2 cup chickpea flour (75g)

1 teaspoon ground cumin

1 teaspoon ground turmeric

3/4 cup water (180ml)

2 medium kumara (800g),
 sliced thickly

vegetable oil, for deep-frying

1 Heat the oil in medium pan;
 cook onion, ginger and garlic,
 stirring, until soft. Add
 tamarind, juice, sugar and
 the water, bring to boil;
 simmer 3 minutes.

2 Stir in tomato; simmer
 about 20 minutes or until
 mixture thickens.

3 Add yabbies; cook, stirring,
 about 5 minutes or until yabbies
 are just changed in colour. Serve
 with spinach and pakoras.

pakoras Combine flours and
spices in medium bowl; stir
in the water, cover, refrigerate
20 minutes. Boil, steam or
microwave kumara until almost
tender; cool, pat dry with
absorbent paper. Coat kumara
in batter. Heat oil in large
pan; deep-fry kumara, in
batches, until browned and
cooked through. Drain on
absorbent paper.

SERVES 4

per serve 7g fat; 1928kJ
(excludes oil for deep-frying)

Adding tamarind to onion mixture

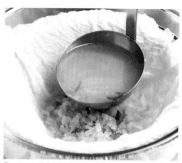

Straining fish stock

1 Combine bones and the water in large pan, bring to the boil, covered; simmer, uncovered, 20 minutes. Strain fish stock over large bowl; discard bones.

2 Heat the oil in large pan; cook brown onion, stirring, until soft. Add celery, lemon grass, lime leaves, chilli, ginger, galangal and sauce; cook, stirring, about 5 minutes or until mixture is fragrant and celery tender. Add reserved fish stock; bring to the boil, simmer, covered, 1 1/2 hours.

3 Strain stock mixture through muslin cloth over large bowl; discard solids.

4 Meanwhile, shell and devein prawns, leaving tails intact (see page 111).

5 Return stock to clean large pan. Bring to the boil, covered; simmer, uncovered, 20 minutes. Add prawns; cook, uncovered, about 5 minutes or until prawns are just changed in colour.

6 Just before serving, stir in sprouts, green onion, coriander and mint.

SERVES 4

per serve 7g fat; 1018kJ

tip Fish stock can be made ahead. Cover; refrigerate or freeze.

BOWL AND SPOON FROM TATTI

tom yum goong

PREPARATION TIME 20 MINUTES • COOKING TIME 2 HOURS

Tom Yum Goong is a traditional sweet and sour soup from Thailand.

1kg fish bones
3 litres cold water (12 cups)
1 tablespoon peanut oil
2 medium brown onions (300g), chopped finely
2 sticks trimmed celery (150g), chopped finely
2 sticks lemon grass, chopped finely
5 kaffir lime leaves, chopped coarsely
4 red Thai chillies, sliced thinly

2 tablespoons grated fresh ginger
1 tablespoon finely grated fresh galangal
2 teaspoons fish sauce
24 large uncooked prawns (1kg)
1 cup bean sprouts (80g)
2 green onions, sliced thinly
1/2 cup loosely packed fresh coriander leaves
1/4 cup loosely packed fresh Vietnamese mint leaves

balmain bug with green mango salad

PREPARATION TIME 20 MINUTES • COOKING TIME 5 MINUTES

With similar flesh to lobster, this shovel-shaped mollusc is found along the south-east coast of Australia. You could substitute prawns or scampi in this recipe. Green mango is the tart, unripe fruit used in India, Malaysia and Thailand.

2 medium green mangoes (860g)
16 cooked Balmain bugs (2kg), prepared (see page 111)
80g trimmed watercress
2 tablespoons thinly sliced lime rind

FRESH MANGO DRESSING
2 small ripe mangoes (600g)
90g palm sugar, chopped finely
2 tablespoons grated ginger
1/3 cup lime juice (80ml)

1 Peel green mangoes; slice off cheeks. Cut mango flesh into 2cm pieces.

2 Combine flesh from bugs in large bowl with mango, watercress and rind; gently toss. Drizzle with dressing to serve.

fresh mango dressing Peel mangoes, slice off cheeks; blend or process mango flesh until smooth. Combine mango puree, sugar, ginger and juice in small pan; cook, stirring, over low heat until sugar dissolves. Bring to boil; simmer, uncovered, about 5 minutes or until dressing thickens slightly. Strain dressing over small bowl; discard solids in sieve, cool.

SERVES 4

per serve 2.8g fat; 1942kJ

tip Mango can be pickled or used fresh in vegetable and lentil dishes. Green mangoes are suitable for chutneys, curries and other oriental dishes.

Shelling and deveining Balmain bug

Cutting mango cheek into pieces

fresh lobster spring rolls

PREPARATION TIME 25 MINUTES • COOKING TIME 5 MINUTES

2 large red capsicums (700g)
4 small cooked lobster
  tails (620g), prepared
  (see page 111)
16 x 22cm rice paper sheets
1 large avocado
  (320g), sliced
1 bunch fresh chives
2 tablespoons lime juice
1/2 teaspoon wasabi
2 tablespoons seasoned
  rice vinegar
1 tablespoon peanut oil

1 Quarter capsicums, discard seeds and membranes. Roast in very hot oven, skin-side up, until skin blisters and blackens. Cover capsicum pieces with plastic or paper for 5 minutes, peel away skin; cut capsicum pieces in half lengthways.

2 Cut each lobster tail lengthways into four equal pieces.

3 Place 1 sheet of rice paper in medium bowl of warm water until just softened; lift from water carefully, place on board. Place a piece of capsicum in centre of rice paper; top with a piece of lobster, avocado slice and a few chives. Roll to enclose; folding in ends (roll should be about 10cm long). Repeat with remaining rice paper sheets, capsicum, lobster, avocado and chives. Cut each roll in half to serve.

4 Combine remaining ingredients in small bowl; serve as a dipping sauce with rolls.

SERVES 4 (MAKES 16 ROLLS)

per serve 19g fat; 1531kJ

PLATTER AND SMALL BOWL FROM EMPIRE HOMEWARES

Covering capsicum with plastic

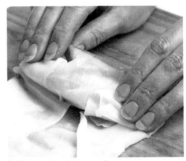

Rolling and enclosing ends

prawn kebabs with chilli lime sauce

PREPARATION TIME 40 MINUTES (PLUS MARINATING TIME) • COOKING TIME 25 MINUTES

32 medium uncooked
   prawns (800g)
2 cloves garlic, crushed
1 tablespoon finely chopped
   fresh lemon grass
1 tablespoon balsamic vinegar
1 tablespoon coarsely chopped
   fresh coriander leaves
1 tablespoon peanut oil
4 green onions

CHILLI LIME SAUCE
²/₃ cup sugar (150g)
¹/₂ cup water (125ml)
1 teaspoon finely grated lime rind
2 red Thai chillies, seeded,
   chopped finely
2 tablespoons sweet chilli sauce
¹/₃ cup lime juice (80ml)

1 Shell and devein prawns, leaving tails intact (see page 111).

2 Combine prawns in medium bowl with garlic, lemon grass, vinegar, coriander and the oil, cover; refrigerate 3 hours or overnight.

3 Drain prawns; discard marinade. Cut onions into 5cm lengths; alternating onion pieces and prawns, thread on 8 skewers. Cook in heated oiled grill pan (or on barbecue or grill) until browned both sides. Serve kebabs with chilli lime sauce.

chilli lime sauce Combine sugar and the water in small pan; stir over heat, without boiling, until sugar dissolves. Simmer, uncovered, without stirring, 5 minutes. Add rind, chilli and sauce; simmer, uncovered, 5 minutes. Stir in juice; cool.

SERVES 4

per serve 5.9g fat; 1328kJ
tip You need to soak the 8 bamboo skewers in water at least 1 hour before using, to avoid scorching.

Threading prawns and onion onto skewers

prawn quesadillas with corn and lime salsa

PREPARATION TIME 30 MINUTES • COOKING TIME 20 MINUTES

Corn tortillas are eaten throughout Mexico while flour tortillas, as a rule, mainly play a role in northern Mexican cuisine. Both types are available either frozen or fresh in most supermarkets.

32 medium uncooked prawns (800g), prepared (see page 111)
2 teaspoons ground cumin
2 teaspoons ground coriander
1/2 teaspoon chilli powder
1 clove garlic, crushed
1 tablespoon peanut oil
3 green onions, chopped finely
100g fetta cheese, crumbled
8 corn tortillas
1/2 cup sour cream (125ml)

CORN AND LIME SALSA

2 corn cobs (500g)
1/4 cup lime juice (60ml)
1 small red onion (100g), chopped finely
4 small tomatoes (520g), seeded, chopped finely
1 medium avocado (250g), chopped
1 tablespoon coarsely chopped fresh coriander leaves

1 Combine prawns in large bowl with cumin, coriander, chilli, garlic and half of the oil.

2 Heat remaining oil in large pan; cook prawn mixture, in batches, until prawns have changed colour. Combine prawn mixture in large bowl with onion and fetta.

3 Soften tortillas in microwave oven, or follow manufacturer's instructions. Divide prawn mixture among tortillas; fold to enclose quesadilla filling.

4 Place quesadillas in batches, seam-side down, in same heated pan; cook, uncovered, until browned both sides and heated through.

5 Serve quesadillas with sour cream and salsa.

corn and lime salsa Cook corn in heated oiled grill pan (or on grill or barbecue) until browned and cooked through. Cut corn kernels from cob; combine in medium bowl with remaining ingredients.

SERVES 4

per serve 33.5g fat; 2563kJ

Deveining prawns

Cutting browned corn from cob

lobster tails with mustard sauce

PREPARATION TIME 25 MINUTES • COOKING TIME 25 MINUTES

10 kipfler potatoes (500g)

2 limes, quartered

**4 small uncooked lobster
  tails (620g)**

1/4 cup seeded mustard (70g)

1/4 cup chopped fresh chives

2 tablespoons white wine vinegar

2 tablespoons olive oil

1 tablespoon salmon roe

1 Boil, steam or microwave potatoes until just tender; halve lengthways. Brown potato halves and lime quarters, in batches, on heated oiled grill plate (or grill or barbecue); cover to keep warm.

2 Remove and discard soft shell from underneath lobster tails to expose flesh. Cut each lobster tail in half lengthways. Cook lobster on heated oiled grill plate (or grill or barbecue) until browned all over and changed in colour.

3 Whisk mustard, chives, vinegar and the oil in small bowl; drizzle dressing over lobster, potato and lime, top with roe.

SERVES 4

per serve 11.6g fat; 1275kJ

tip You can serve lobsters either in or out of their shells.

Grilling potato and lime

Cutting lobster tail

scampi with risotto triangles

PREPARATION TIME 30 MINUTES (PLUS REFRIGERATION TIME) • COOKING TIME 50 MINUTES

24 uncooked scampi (1.2kg)

¹/₂ cup olive oil (125ml)

3 teaspoons finely grated lemon rind

¹/₃ cup lemon juice (80ml)

¹/₂ teaspoon cracked black pepper

2 tablespoons chopped fresh dill

100g rocket, trimmed

RISOTTO TRIANGLES

¹/₄ cup olive oil (60ml)

1 medium brown onion (150g), chopped finely

1 cup arborio rice (200g)

¹/₂ cup dry white wine (125ml)

3 cups hot vegetable stock (750ml)

¹/₂ cup finely grated parmesan cheese (40g)

plain flour

1 Prepare scampi, discard head, leaving meat in shell (see page 111).

2 Combine the oil, rind, juice, pepper and dill in jug. Place scampi in large bowl; pour over one-third of the marinade.

3 Cook scampi in large heated pan, stirring, about 3 minutes or until cooked through. Serve scampi, on rocket, with risotto triangles; drizzle with reserved marinade.

risotto triangles Coat 23cm-square slab cake pan with cooking-oil spray; line base and two sides with baking paper, extending paper 2cm above edge of pan. Heat 1 tablespoon of the oil in medium pan; cook onion, stirring, until soft. Add rice; stir to coat with oil. Add wine; cook, stirring, until wine is absorbed. Stir in stock; cook, uncovered, stirring occasionally, about 20 minutes or until rice is just tender and liquid absorbed. Stir in cheese. Press risotto into prepared pan; cover, refrigerate 3 hours or overnight. Cut risotto into four squares, cut each square into four triangles; coat triangles in flour, shake off excess. Heat remaining oil in large pan; cook risotto triangles, in batches, until browned both sides and heated through. Drain on absorbent paper.

SERVES 4

per serve 51g fat; 3658kJ

Scampi in bowl with marinade

Pressing risotto into lined cake tin

sichuan-style prawns with rice noodles

PREPARATION TIME 20 MINUTES • COOKING TIME 15 MINUTES

The seeds that come from the eight segments of the star anise are one of the main ingredients of five-spice powder.

40 medium uncooked prawns (1kg)
2 tablespoons Sichuan peppercorns
4 star anise
1 teaspoon sea salt
420g fresh rice noodles
1 tablespoon peanut oil
400g baby bok choy, trimmed, chopped roughly
500g choy sum, trimmed, chopped roughly
1/3 cup oyster sauce (80ml)
1 tablespoon soy sauce

1 Shell and devein prawns, leaving tails intact (see page 111).

2 Crush peppercorns, star anise and salt; coat prawns in spice mix.

3 Place noodles in large bowl, cover with warm water; gently separate noodles with hands. Soak noodles 1 minute; drain, rinse under cold water, drain.

4 Heat half of the oil in wok; stir-fry prawns, in batches, until just changed in colour. Heat remaining oil in same wok; stir-fry noodles, bok choy, choy sum and sauces, tossing, until noodles are hot and vegetables just wilted. Serve noodles topped with prawns.

SERVES 4

per serve 2.7g fat; 1181kJ

tip To crush peppercorns, you can use a mortar and pestle, a spice grinder, blender, food processor or meat mallet.

Crushing spices with mortar and pestle

Separating noodles in bowl

seafood preparation

...our expert demonstrates some simple techniques

cleaning fish cut fish open, as shown; remove and discard entrails.

filleting a round fish *(such as bream, snapper and luderick)* cut halfway through fish along front fin.

scaling fish hold fish firmly by the tail. Use blunt knife to remove scales, working from tail to head.

Starting at head of fish, cut flat against spine; move knife along spine towards tail with a gentle press-and-push motion.

skinning fillets cut a little of the flesh from the skin at tail end of fillet. Hold the skin with salted fingers at tail end and continue cutting away flesh, keeping knife flat against the skin.

Picture shows rib cage and fillet cut away. Turn fish over, repeat on other side.

filleting a flat fish cut through centre of fish along spine, from head towards tail.

Carefully cut flesh away from fish, scraping blade of knife along bones as you cut.

skinning a whole flat fish nick skin at tail end of fish, use salt on fingers to give grip. Hold fish firmly by the tail, pull skin in opposite direction.

boning whole fish remove head. Cut through flesh from gills to tail, along belly. Cut through flesh on either side of backbone so fish can be spread out flat; avoid cutting into the skin.

Spread fish out flat, cut out backbone using scissors or knife.

Spread fish out flat, trim off rib bones on each side.

butterflying garfish and sardines cut off heads and remove entrails.

Cut through underside to backbone; rinse under cold water. Cut through backbone at tail end without piercing skin. Pull backbone out towards head end to remove. Remove small bones.

Butterflied fish with bones removed.

shelling prawns and scampi

note: *some recipes require head and tail, or just tail, to be left on.*

The same method is used whether they are cooked or uncooked. To remove head, hold head firmly and twist body of prawn.

Remove legs and shell from body without removing tail shell.

To remove tail, first break off the two tail fins.

Slip tail shell from prawn.

Remove back vein from prawn (even if head and tail remain on).

preparing cooked lobsters (crayfish), marrons or yabbies

place lobster with back down, cut through chest and tail.

Turn lobster around and cut through head.

Pull lobster halves apart. Discard white gills and grey thread running down centre back of tail. The liver or creamy green part can be used to make sauce. Use fingers to remove meat from tail sections.

preparing cooked balmain bugs

place back down. Cut tail from body.

Cut through tail lengthways.

Remove back vein from tail.

Remove meat from tail halves.

shucking oysters insert strong, short-bladed, rigid knife (oyster knife) next to hinge between the two shells. Twist knife to pop shell open.

Remove top shell, loosen oyster with knife. Turn oyster over and return to washed and dried shell for serving.

preparing mussels for cooking to clean mussels, pull away the seaweed thread or "beard". Use a stiff brush to scrub shells under cold water. Boil, steam or microwave to open. ***Note:*** *1kg mussels in shells yields 250g meat.*

preparing clams and pipis live clams and pipis are often sold "sand-free" and need no preparation. To clean clams or pipis, scrub shells with stiff brush if necessary, then soak in lightly salted water for a few hours; stir occasionally, or change the water, to encourage them to discard their sand.

preparing cuttlefish gently cut through to centre of cuttlefish on soft side, to avoid breaking the black ink sac. The ink sac is edible, but it can be messy if spilt. Rinse away under cold running water. Gently pull head and tentacles from body.

Remove cuttle bone from body. Firmly pull skin away from meat, wash meat well.

Cut into slices or cut diamond pattern into cuttlefish pieces without cutting right through (known as honeycombing).

preparing octopus cut head from tentacles just below eyes.

Cut eyes away from head, discard eyes. Remove body "beak" from centre of legs by pushing finger through centre; beak should pop out. Discard beak.

Pull skin gently away from head; wash head and tentacles thoroughly.

preparing squid gently pull head and entrails away from body of squid. Remove clear backbone (quill) from inside body.

Cut tentacles from head just below eyes; discard head. Remove side flaps and skin from squid hood with salted fingers. Pull firmly. Wash hood, tentacles and flaps thoroughly. Cut hood into rings, or use whole. Cut tentacles into pieces and flaps into strips.

removing meat from crabs cooked and uncooked crabs are handled in the same way. To kill crabs humanely see page 116. Hold crab firmly. Slide sharp, strong knife under top of shell at back, lever off shell.

Remove and discard whitish gills. Rinse well under cold water. Cut crab body in quarters or as required.

Remove meat from shell with fingers.

Use meat mallet or nutcracker to break claws; remove meat.

glossary

kaffir lime

Bacon rashers also known as slices of bacon.

Beetroot also known as beets.

Bok choy also called pak choi or Chinese white cabbage.

Bread
PIDE Turkish wheat-flour bread that comes in long flat loaves as well as individual rounds.
PITTA Lebanese wheat-flour pocket bread, also spelled pita. Sold in large, flat rounds.

Breadcrumbs
PACKAGED fine-textured, crunchy, white breadcrumbs.
STALE made by grating or processing day-old bread.

Caperberries fruit formed after caper buds have flowered; caperberries are pickled.

Capers the buds of a warm-climate shrub; sold dried and salted, or pickled in brine.

Capsicum also known as bell pepper or, simply, pepper.

Celeriac tuberous root with white flesh; celery flavoured.

Cheese
FETTA a crumbly-textured goat or sheep milk cheese.
HALOUMI a firm sheep milk cheese matured in brine.
MASCARPONE a fresh, triple-cream cheese with a sweet, slightly sour taste.
PARMESAN a dry, hard cheese, made from skim or part-skim milk and aged at least a year.

Chermoulla Spicy Moroccan paste mixture including coriander, cumin and paprika.

Chickpeas also called channa, garbanzos or hummus; round, sandy-coloured legume.

Chillies use rubber gloves when chopping fresh chillies as they can burn your skin. Removing seeds lessens the heat level.
DRIED, CRUSHED buy in Asian food stores and supermarkets.
JALAPEÑO hot green chillies, available in brine or fresh from greengrocers.

POWDER made from ground chillies; substitute 1/2 teaspoon chilli powder for 1 medium chopped fresh chilli.
SWEET CHILLI SAUCE a mild, Thai sauce made from red chillies, sugar, garlic and vinegar.
THAI green or red in colour, they are small, hot chillies.

Coconut
CREAM made from coconut flesh and water; sold in cans and cartons. Thicker and richer than coconut milk.
DESICCATED concentrated, dried, shredded coconut.
MILK unsweetened coconut milk available in cans.

Coriander also known as cilantro or Chinese parsley.

Couscous a grain-like cereal product made from semolina.

Crème fraîche velvety cream with tangy taste (has minimum fat content of 35%).

Cucumber, Lebanese slender and thin-skinned; also known as the European or burpless cucumber.

Dashi Japanese stock made from dried bonito flakes and kelp; instant dashi powder is available. Sold in Asian specialty stores.

Eggplant also known as aubergine.

Eggs some recipes use raw or barely-cooked eggs; show caution if salmonella is a problem in your area.

Five-spice powder fragrant, ground mixture of cinnamon, cloves, star anise, Sichuan pepper and fennel seeds.

Flour
BUCKWHEAT made from roasted buckwheat seeds.
CHICKPEA made from ground chickpeas; also known as garam flour or besan.
PLAIN all-purpose wheat flour.
SELF-RAISING plain flour sifted with baking powder in ratio of 1 cup flour to 2 level teaspoons baking powder.

Galangal member of the ginger family; the piquant, fibrous root is sold fresh or ground. Also known as laos.

Garam masala a blend of spices including cardamom, cinnamon, clove, coriander, fennel, cumin, and sometimes black pepper and chilli.

Ginger
FRESH also known as green or root ginger; the thick gnarled root of a tropical plant.
GROUND also known as powdered ginger; cannot be substituted for fresh ginger.
PICKLED Thin, pink shavings of ginger pickled in vinegar, sugar and natural colouring.
RED PICKLED also called Chinese ginger; preserved ginger shreds in heavy, slightly salty syrup.

Ghee clarified butter, with the milk solids removed.

Gremolata an Italian garnish of finely chopped garlic, fresh parsley and lemon rind.

Herbs when specified, we used dried (not ground) herbs in the ratio of 1:4 for fresh herbs.

Horseradish
CREAM a paste of vinegar, oil, sugar and grated horseradish.
FRESH a plant whose root has a hot, pungent flavour.
PREPARED grated horseradish with flavourings; do not confuse with horseradish cream.

Kaffir lime wrinkly green fruit of a small citrus tree.

Kaffir lime leaves leaves of citrus tree; used fresh or dried.

Ketjap manis Indonesian sweet, thick soy sauce.

Kitchen string string made for use in cooking; synthetic string will melt near heat.

Kumara Polynesian name of orange-fleshed sweet potato.

Laksa spicy soup of noodles, seafood or chicken, and coconut cream.

Laksa paste bottled paste containing lemon grass, chillies, galangal, shrimp paste, onions and turmeric.

Lemon grass lemon-tasting, sharp-edged grass; the white lower stem is used. Strips of lemon zest can be substituted.

Lemon myrtle if packaged ground lemon myrtle is unavailable, substitute a

mixture of fresh lemon grass, lime rind and lemon rind.

Mirin a sweet low-alcohol rice wine used in Japanese cooking; do not confuse with sake.

Miso Japanese paste of salted, fermented soy beans; used in soups, sauces, dressings.

Mushrooms
CUP have full-bodied flavour and firm texture.
FLAT large, soft and flat, with a rich earthy flavour.
SHIITAKE also called Chinese black mushrooms.

Mustard
DIJON a pale brown, fairly-mild French mustard.
FRENCH plain mild mustard.
SEEDED a coarse-grain mustard, also known as wholegrain.

Noodles
DRIED RICE STICK there are two varieties, flat and thin, made from rice flour and water.
FRESH EGG made from wheat flour and eggs.
FRESH RICE thick, wide, almost white in colour; made from rice and vegetable oil. Cover with boiling water, drain, before using.
RICE VERMICELLI also known as rice-flour or rice-stick noodles; sold dried.

Nori dried seaweed; sold in thin sheets, toasted or plain. Used for sushi or as a garnish.

Nuts
MACADAMIA rich and buttery nut; store in refrigerator.
PECAN golden-brown, rich nut.
PINE also known as pignoli; small, cream-coloured kernels from certain pine cones.
PISTACHIO pale green, delicately-flavoured nut inside hard off-white shells.
WALNUT sold in the shell or shelled (whole or pieces).

Oil
CHILLI made by steeping red chillies in vegetable oil.
COOKING-OIL SPRAY vegetable oil in an aerosol can.
CORN an odourless, bland oil; has a high smoke point.
MACADAMIA mono-unsaturated oil extracted from macadamias.

preserved lemon

capers

tiny capers

caperberries

PEANUT used in Asian cooking; has high smoke point.

SESAME made from white sesame seeds; used to flavour.

VEGETABLE oils sourced from plants rather than animal fats.

Olive oil

EXTRA VIRGIN AND VIRGIN best-quality olive oils, obtained from first pressings of olives.

OLIVE made from the pressing of tree-ripened olives. Extra Light or Light describes the mild flavour, not fat levels.

Onion

GREEN also known as scallion or (incorrectly) shallot; onion picked before bulb has formed. Has long, green edible stalk.

RED also known as Spanish or Bermuda onion; sweet-flavoured, good eaten raw in salads.

SPRING has narrow, green top and sweet, white bulb.

Paprika ground, dried, red capsicum; sweet or hot.

Parsley, flat-leaf also known as continental parsley or Italian parsley.

Potatoes

KIPFLER small and finger-shaped, with a nutty flavour; good baked.

TINY (BABY) NEW also known as chats. Potato harvested young; has waxy, paper-thin skin.

Preserved lemon a North African specialty; lemons quartered and preserved in salt and lemon juice. To use, discard pulp, squeeze juice from rind, rinse rind; slice. Sold in delicatessens; keep in refrigerator.

Prosciutto cured, air-dried (unsmoked), pressed ham, sold thinly sliced.

Puy lentils small, dark-green, fast-cooking lentils with a delicate flavour. Originally from Le Puy, France.

Rice

ARBORIO large, round-grain rice; used for risottos.

BASMATI a white, fragrant, long-grain rice. It should be washed before cooking.

BROWN natural whole grain.

CALROSE medium-grain rice.

JASMINE fragrant long-grain rice; substitute white long-grain rice.

KOSHIHIKARI small, round-grain white rice. Substitute white short-grain rice and cook by the absorption method.

LONG-GRAIN elongated grains, stay separate when cooked.

SHORT-GRAIN fat, almost-round grain with high starch content.

WILD not a true member of the rice family, this blackish-brown seed has a distinctive flavour; is also blended with white rice.

Rice paper also known as banh trang. Made from rice paste; stamped into rounds. Dipped in warm water they become pliable food wrappers.

Rind also known as zest.

Rocket also known as arugula, rucola, rugula; salad leaf.

Saffron stigma of a type of crocus; available in strands or ground. Store in the freezer.

Score shallow cuts, usually in criss-cross pattern.

Sauces

BARBECUE tomato-based sauce used to marinate and baste.

FISH also called nam pla or nuoc nam; made from salted, pulverised, fermented fish.

HOISIN thick, sweet, Chinese paste made from fermented soy beans, onions and garlic.

OYSTER rich, brown sauce based on oysters and their brine.

SOY made from fermented soy beans.

SWEET CHILLI see entry under chillies.

TABASCO brand name of fiery sauce made from vinegar, hot red peppers and salt.

WORCESTERSHIRE a dark, spicy sauce used as a seasoning.

Seeds

CUMIN also known as zeera.

FENNEL light aniseed-flavour.

Sichuan pepper also known as Szechuan or Chinese pepper. Small, red-brown seeds; with a peppery-lemon flavour.

Snow peas also known as mange tout ("eat all").

Snow pea shoots also known as pea shoots; the young, growing tips of the plant.

Soba thin noodles made from buckwheat and wheat flour.

Spinach, English delicate, green leaves on thin stems; do not mistake for the dark-green, crinkly-leafed silverbeet (also known as Swiss chard or seakale).

Sprouts we use mostly mung bean or alfalfa sprouts.

Star anise dried star-shaped pod; seeds taste of aniseed.

Sugar we used coarse table sugar, also known as crystal sugar, unless otherwise stated.

BROWN a fine, granulated sugar retaining molasses.

CASTER also known as superfine or finely granulated table sugar.

PALM also known as gur, gula jawa, gula melaka and jaggery. Substitute brown or black sugar.

Tamarind

DRIED the red-brown pulp, seeds, rind and fibres of the pod of the tamarind tree. To use, soak in boiling water. When cool, press through a sieve back into the water. Use the liquid; discard pulp.

PULP the dehydrated meat of the tamarind tree's pod; reconstitute as above.

CONCENTRATE thick, purple-black, ready-to-use paste.

Tomato

CANNED whole peeled tomatoes in natural juices.

CHERRY also known as Tiny Tim or Tom Thumb tomatoes.

EGG also called plum or Roma tomatoes; small, oval-shaped.

PASTE triple-concentrated tomato puree.

PUREE canned, pureed tomatoes (not tomato paste).

SAUCE also known as ketchup; flavoured condiment.

SEMI-DRIED egg tomatoes, roasted slowly, available from delicatessens.

Tortilla unleavened bread sold frozen, fresh or vacuum-packed; made from wheat flour or corn (maizemeal).

Turmeric from the ginger family; its dried, ground root gives a rich colour and pungent, but not hot, flavour.

Vietnamese mint narrow-leafed, pungent herb, also known as Cambodian mint and laksa leaf.

Vine leaves grape vine leaves; available fresh or in brine. If fresh, simmer in water for 5 to 10 minutes before using. If brined, rinse well before using.

Vinegar

BALSAMIC authentic only from Modena, Italy; made from a sweet regional white wine aged in antique wooden casks.

RED WINE based on fermented red wine.

RICE made from fermented rice. Substitute diluted cider vinegar or white wine vinegar.

RICE WINE made from fermented rice; use mirin as a substitute.

WHITE made from spirit of cane sugar.

WHITE WINE made from white wine.

Wasabi an Asian horseradish used to make a fiery sauce. Sold as powder or paste.

Watercress dark-green leaves with a bitter, peppery flavour.

Witlof also known as chicory or Belgian endive.

Yeast 7g (1/4oz) of dried yeast (2 teaspoons) equals 15g (1/2oz) compressed yeast if using one for the other.

Zucchini also known as courgette.

puy lentils

seafood guide

buying, freezing and storing tips

WHOLE FISH

TO BUY choose fish with clear bulging eyes and very black pupils, firm lustrous skin with tight scales, bright red gills and a pleasant sea smell.

TO FREEZE gill and gut fish, and wrap carefully in foil (avoid piercing foil). Place into freezer bag, remove air, seal, date and label. Freeze white fish for up to 6 months; 3 months for oily fish.

TO STORE remove scales and wash cavity well, scraping any blood from backbone. Gently shake off excess water, place fish into an airtight container or on a plate, cover with plastic wrap. Refrigerate for up to 3 days.

FISH FILLETS AND CUTLETS

TO BUY flesh should have a slightly shiny surface, be firm (not spongy) and have a pleasant sea smell.

TO FREEZE quickly and gently rinse under cold water, shake off excess water, then wrap each piece individually in freezer wrap and stack in appropriate serving portions.

when shopping for fresh seafood use a chiller bag or esky, or you can ask your fishmonger to pack ice with your purchase

Place portions into freezer bag, remove air, seal, date and label. Freeze white fish for up to 6 months; 3 months for oily fish.

TO STORE quickly and gently rinse fish in cold water, then shake off excess water; place fish in an airtight container or on a plate, and cover with plastic wrap. Refrigerate for up to 3 days.

SMOKED FISH

TO BUY flesh should be firm with a pleasant smell; avoid fish with a sticky surface.

TO FREEZE as for fresh fish, but saltiness can increase during freezing and smoked flavour may decrease. Freeze for up to 3 months.

TO STORE place in airtight container or wrap in foil. Refrigerate up to 5 days.

PRAWNS AND SCAMPI

TO BUY sold cooked or uncooked (known as green). When cooked they are orange in colour. Shells should be firmly intact and have a pleasant sea smell.

TO FREEZE cooked and uncooked, they are best frozen in their shells. Place in container, barely cover with tap water, allowing space for water to expand during freezing, seal and freeze like an ice block for up to 3 months. To defrost, place under cold running water to melt the ice, then refrigerate prawns for several hours or until they reach edible temperature.

TO STORE cooked and uncooked, rinse quickly under cold water then shake off excess water; place unshelled into airtight container or onto a plate, and cover with plastic wrap. Refrigerate up to 3 days.

OTHER CRUSTACEANS

(lobsters/crayfish, Balmain bugs, crabs, yabbies, marron)

TO BUY these are available cooked, uncooked and live. When cooked, they are orange in colour with no black discolouration, particularly at the joints. Shells should be firmly intact (lobster tails should be curled) and have a pleasant sea smell. When uncooked, they are known as "green" though they may sometimes be another colour, such as the blue swimmer crabs. Shells should be firm and have a pleasant sea smell. When live, look for active animals for freshest flavour. These must be killed as humanely as possible. We recommend drowning in fresh water or freezing for 2 hours (any longer will freeze the meat), or putting them in a container of iced water for 1/2 hour before cooking. Use as directed in recipes. We do not recommend cooking live animals as it is unnecessarily cruel, and will toughen the meat and cause claws and nippers to snap off.

TO FREEZE cooked and uncooked, they should be cleaned well then wrapped (still in their shells) in foil (avoid piercing foil). Place into freezer bag, remove air, seal, date and label. Freeze for up to 3 months.

TO STORE cooked and uncooked, follow guide for prawns and scampi.

SHELLFISH

(mussels, pipis, oysters, clams, cockles, etc.)

TO BUY molluscs should have a pleasant sea smell and be firmly closed (except for the green-lipped New Zealand mussels).

TO FREEZE not recommended.

TO STORE place molluscs into colander, cover with a damp cloth, then place colander

into a slightly larger bowl; place in the lowest section of refrigerator, use within 3 days.

TO COOK wash and scrub shells (remove fibrous beards from mussels by pulling firmly). Follow recipe instructions for cooking. As shells open, remove from heat. Shells that do not open when most have opened can be prised open with a blunt knife. If the meat is firm and intact and smells good, include it with the rest. It was previously thought that all unopened molluscs should be discarded, but it is now known that some shells do not open because the meat is attached on both sides.

OTHER MOLLUSCS

(squid/calamari, octopus and cuttlefish)

TO BUY choose those with a mottled brown skin; avoid any with a dark purple-black colouring.

TO FREEZE gut, clean and wash well. Wrap in freezer wrap, place in freezer bag, remove air, seal, date and label. Freeze up to 3 months.

TO STORE rinse quickly under cold water, shake off excess water; place into an airtight container or on a plate, and cover with plastic wrap. Refrigerate for up to 3 days. These can be cleaned and prepared before storing, if preferred.

TO COOK these go through a cooking cycle of tender to tough then back to tender. All require very quick cooking (for example, 1 minute for cuttlefish and squid and 3 to 4 minutes for octopus) to be tender. Alternatively, depending on individual recipe, if the heat is lowered to simmer and cooking time extended to about 45 minutes, the flesh will tenderise again.

index

microwave oven tips

• To prevent overcooking, careful timing and checking is important when microwaving seafood. Fish is cooked when opaque or white in colour. Cover fish during cooking.

• Fold thin tail ends under fillets to give uniform thickness in microwave oven.

• Arrange fish and shellfish with the thickest parts towards the outer edge of the microwave turntable.

• Avoid stacking seafood; a single layer of food will ensure more even and faster cooking.

• When microwaving pieces of fish, MEDIUM-HIGH (70%) power is usually enough. Whole fish can be given up to 3 minutes on HIGH (100%). Shellfish and molluscs which are protected by a shell can be microwaved on HIGH (100%).

• Pierce eyes of whole fish and cover the thinner tail ends with lightly greased foil for half the cooking time, to prevent overcooking.

• Use a knife to cut slashes in thick parts of whole fish or fish fillets, to allow more even cooking.

• Always allow up to 2 minutes standing time for fish after microwaving, to complete the cooking.

make your own stock

These recipes can be made up to 4 days ahead and stored, covered, in the refrigerator. Be sure to remove any fat from the surface after the cooled stock has been refrigerated overnight. If the stock is to be kept longer, it is best to freeze it in smaller quantities. *All stock recipes make about 2.5 litres (10 cups).*

Stock is also available in cans or tetra packs. Stock cubes or powder can be used. As a guide, 1 teaspoon of stock powder or 1 small crumbled stock cube mixed with 1 cup (250ml) water will give a fairly strong stock. Be aware of the salt and fat content of stock cubes and powders and prepared stocks.

CHICKEN STOCK

2kg chicken bones
2 medium onions (300g), chopped
2 sticks celery, chopped
2 medium carrots (250g), chopped
3 bay leaves
2 teaspoons black peppercorns
5 litres water (20 cups)

Combine all ingredients in large pan, simmer, uncovered, 2 hours; strain.

FISH STOCK

1.5kg fish bones
3 litres water (12 cups)
1 medium onion (150g), chopped
2 sticks celery, chopped
2 bay leaves
1 teaspoon black peppercorns

Combine all ingredients in large pan, simmer, uncovered, 20 minutes; strain.

VEGETABLE STOCK

2 large carrots (360g), chopped
2 large parsnips (360g), chopped
4 medium onions (600g), chopped
12 sticks celery, chopped
4 bay leaves
2 teaspoons black peppercorns
6 litres water (24 cups)

Combine all ingredients in large pan, simmer, uncovered, 1½ hours; strain.

facts and figures

Wherever you live, you'll be able to use our recipes with the help of these easy-to-follow conversions. While these conversions are approximate only, the difference between an exact and the approximate conversion of various liquid and dry measures is but minimal and will not affect your cooking results.

dry measures

metric	imperial
15g	1/2oz
30g	1oz
60g	2oz
90g	3oz
125g	4oz (1/4lb)
155g	5oz
185g	6oz
220g	7oz
250g	8oz (1/2lb)
280g	9oz
315g	10oz
345g	11oz
375g	12oz (3/4lb)
410g	13oz
440g	14oz
470g	15oz
500g	16oz (1lb)
750g	24oz (1 1/2lb)
1kg	32oz (2lb)

liquid measures

metric	imperial
30ml	1 fluid oz
60ml	2 fluid oz
100ml	3 fluid oz
125ml	4 fluid oz
150ml	5 fluid oz (1/4 pint/1 gill)
190ml	6 fluid oz
250ml	8 fluid oz
300ml	10 fluid oz (1/2 pint)
500ml	16 fluid oz
600ml	20 fluid oz (1 pint)
1000ml (1 litre)	1 3/4 pints

helpful measures

metric	imperial
3mm	1/8in
6mm	1/4in
1cm	1/2in
2cm	3/4in
2.5cm	1in
5cm	2in
6cm	2 1/2in
8cm	3in
10cm	4in
13cm	5in
15cm	6in
18cm	7in
20cm	8in
23cm	9in
25cm	10in
28cm	11in
30cm	12in (1ft)

helpful measures

The difference between one country's measuring cups and another's is, at most, within a 2 or 3 teaspoon variance. (For the record, 1 Australian metric measuring cup holds approximately 250ml.) The most accurate way of measuring dry ingredients is to weigh them. When measuring liquids, use a clear glass or plastic jug with the metric markings. (One Australian metric tablespoon holds 20ml; one Australian metric teaspoon holds 5ml.)

If you would like to purchase *The Australian Women's Weekly* Test Kitchen's metric measuring cups and spoons (as approved by Standards Australia), turn to page 120 for details and order coupon. You will receive:

- a graduated set of 4 cups for measuring dry ingredients, with sizes marked on the cups.
- a graduated set of 4 spoons for measuring dry and liquid ingredients, with amounts marked on the spoons.

Note: North America, NZ and the UK use 15ml tablespoons. All cup and spoon measurements are level.

We use large eggs having an average weight of 60g.

oven temperatures

These oven temperatures are only a guide. Always check the manufacturer's manual.

	C° (Celsius)	F° (Fahrenheit)	Gas Mark
Very slow	120	250	1
Slow	150	300	2
Moderately slow	160	325	3
Moderate	180 - 190	350 - 375	4
Moderately hot	200 - 210	400 - 425	5
Hot	220 - 230	450 - 475	6
Very hot	240 - 250	500 - 525	7

how to measure

When using graduated metric measuring cups, shake dry ingredients loosely into the appropriate cup. Do not tap the cup on a bench or tightly pack the ingredients unless directed to do so. Level top of measuring cups and measuring spoons with a knife. When measuring liquids, place a clear glass or plastic jug with metric markings on a flat surface to check accuracy at eye level.

Looking after your interest...

Keep your Home Library cookbooks clean, tidy and within easy reach with slipcovers designed to hold up to 12 books. *Plus* you can follow our recipes perfectly with a set of accurate measuring cups and spoons, as used by *The Australian Women's Weekly* Test Kitchen.

TO ORDER

Mail or fax Photocopy or complete the coupon below and post to AWW Home Library Reader Offer, ACP Direct, PO Box 7036, Sydney NSW 1028, *or* fax to (02) 9267 4363.

Credit cards Have your details ready then, if you live in Sydney, phone 9260 0000; if you live elsewhere in Australia, phone 1800 252 515 (free call, Mon-Fri, 8.30am-5.30pm).

PRICE

Book Holder $11.95 (Australia); elsewhere $A21.95.

Metric Measuring Set $5.95 (Australia); $A8.00 (New Zealand); $A9.95 elsewhere. Prices include postage and handling. This offer is available in all countries.

PAYMENT

Australian residents We accept the credit cards listed on the coupon, money orders and cheques.

Overseas residents We accept the credit cards listed on the coupon, drafts in $A drawn on an Australian bank, and also British, New Zealand and U.S. cheques in the currency of the country of issue. Credit card charges are at the exchange rate current at the time of payment.

☐ BOOK HOLDER   ☐ METRIC MEASURING SET

Please indicate number(s) required.

Mr/Mrs/Ms _____

Address _____

_____

Postcode _____ Country _____

Ph: Bus. Hours:(   ) _____

I enclose my cheque/money order for $_____ payable to ACP Direct

OR: please charge my

☐ Bankcard ☐ Visa ☐ MasterCard ☐ Diners Club ☐ Amex

☐☐☐☐☐☐☐☐☐☐☐☐☐☐☐☐☐☐☐☐

Expiry Date ____/____

Cardholder's signature _____

Please allow up to 30 days for delivery within Australia. Allow up to 6 weeks for overseas deliveries. Both offers expire 31/05/00.
HLESFD99